★ ★ ★

ADVANCE PRAISE

★ ★ ★

"I really enjoyed reading it! Peter Walker has done a wonderful job
in laying out the cultural, philosophical and historical foundations
for both countries and comparing them side by side."

Catherine Mengyun Yang, TIE-SEI Fellow,
The Fletcher School of Law and Diplomacy, Tufts University

"The timing of writing on this subject is perfect and the approach
that Peter Walker takes in comparing the two cultures/histories
is very enlightening ... An important read."

Claude Dussault, Chairman, Intact Financial Corporation

"Peter Walker has written a brilliant book about China and America.
Walker's accurate descriptions of the differences in 'worldview'
between the US and China are exactly what the US needs to
understand China and for China to better understand the US."

Richard N. Foster, Author of *Innovation:
The Attacker's Advantage* and *Creative Destruction*

"*Powerful, Different, Equal* makes the formerly mysterious
so easy to understand."

Deanna Mulligan, CEO, Guardian Life Insurance

Published by
LID Publishing Limited
The Record Hall, Studio 304,
16-16a Baldwins Gardens,
London EC1N 7RJ, UK

info@lidpublishing.com
www.lidpublishing.com

A member of:

BPR

businesspublishersroundtable.com

© Peter B. Walker, 2020
© LID Publishing Limited, 2020
First edition published in 2019

Printed by CPI Group (UK) Ltd, Croydon CR0 4YY
ISBN: 978-1-911671-40-4

Cover and page design: Caroline Li

PETER B. WALKER

★ ★ ★

POWERFUL DIFFERENT EQUAL

★ ★ ★

OVERCOMING THE MISCONCEPTIONS AND DIFFERENCES BETWEEN CHINA AND THE US

MADRID | MEXICO CITY | LONDON
NEW YORK | BUENOS AIRES
BOGOTA | SHANGHAI | NEW DELHI

To Francine, my rock. Kimberly and Sarah,
who did much of the heavy lifting, and Pamela
and Janet, who are always there for me.

CONTENTS

⋆ ⋆ ⋆

* * *

ACKNOWLEDGMENTS

* * *

Writing this book was a family affair, with Francine always pushing for balance, Kimberly streamlining and sharpening the prose, and Sarah tracking down the facts and the sources.

A special thanks to Catherine Yang, a student at the Fletcher School who spearheaded much of the research. Also, a big thank you to many friends and former colleagues who provided helpful input on the structure and tone of the book, including Andreas Beroutsos, Alan Colberg, Jim Crownover, Claude Dessault, Zach Dykehouse, Dick Foster, Tom Hardy, Paul Mas, Bill Meehan, Deanna Mulligan, David O'Brien, Ron O'Hanley, Hank Walker and Catherine Yang.

A final thank you to my publisher, LID Publishing, for helping a first time author get off the ground – Martin Liu, Susan Furber, Maria Cid and Francesca Stainer.

★ ★ ★

PREFACE FOR THE 2020 EDITION

★ ★ ★

Since the summer of 2019, when my book *Powerful, Different, Equal* was first published in the UK, the US-China relationship has deteriorated. The implementation of Phase 1 of the Trade Deal is being questioned. After first impacting China, Covid-19 spread globally and continues to take a heavy toll on global health and the economy, particularly within the US, where the Trump administration publicly blames China for the devasting virus. US interference with Chinese technology giant Huawei is escalating, including sales interruptions of critical chips to the Chinese company. China is also installing its mainland security apparatus in Hong Kong, inciting anger and likely provoking more demonstrations.

Let's first take a look at the trade front. Phase 1 of the Trade Deal demands from China to:

- Purchase an additional $200 billion in US goods, including manufacturing, energy, services and agricultural goods, over its 2017 purchases
- Agree to strengthen IP protection on patents, trademarks and copyrights, as well as stop requiring forced IT transfer as a condition for market entry
- Suspend retaliatory tariffs on automobile imports
- Further open its domestic market of financial services to foreign competitors
- Commit not to devaluate its currency to improve its trade position

In exchange, the US will cut tariffs from 15% to 7.5% on $120 billion in Chinese imports and suspend indefinitely the tariff increase on the $160 billion in Chinese imports due to be implemented on 15 December 2020.

The Trump administration broadly publicized the contents of Phase 1 as a major breakthrough in US-China relations and promised further breakthroughs in Phases 2 and 3 to be negotiated after the 2020 US presidential election. Independent observers qualify Phase 1 as a purely tactical quid pro quo, with no winner or loser. The core issue of China's centrally managed economy, which is controlled through industry and company specific subsidies, isn't addressed in Phase 1 and likely won't be resolved in Phases 2 and 3. This helps explain why negotiating Phase 2 and 3 is pushed beyond the 2020 election date. While the Trump administration initially asserted trade wars are "good and easy to win," the real result is slower GDP growth within both countries. The hope of repatriation of US manufacturing jobs has not materialized; some American companies are simply redirecting parts of their supply chain to low-cost South East Asian countries like the Philippines, Vietnam, Cambodia and Thailand. Looking forward, the real question isn't the contents of Phases 2 and 3, but whether Phase 1 will be fully implemented.

The Covid-19 outbreak is the most significant development in US-China relations. Originating in Wuhan, China, in late 2019, the virus has now spread globally. While the US accused China of concealing early stages of the outbreak and not doing enough to contain its worldwide spread, the story is a bit more complicated. Covid-19 began with a report of a cluster of pneumonia cases of unknown origin to the Wuhan Municipal Health authorities on 31 December 2019. On 1 January 2020, the World Health Organization (WHO) set up an Incident Management Support Team, treating the outbreak as an emergency. By late January, a team of WHO and Beijing experts had visited Wuhan, ceased all transportation in and out, and completely locked down the city. China's decisive and prompt actions helped limit the outbreak domestically and keep the estimated death toll to less than 5,000 people.

In the US, comparative inaction and a failure to take the threat seriously after the initial outbreak in late January led to a death toll of over 100,000 by late May 2020. In an effort to deflect criticism of its failure to act, the Trump administration launched a significant smear campaign, blaming China for the crisis as well as criticizing and threatening the WHO with a full stop of US funding. The WHO's 194 member states rallied in the organization's defense, initiating a study on lessons learned and effectively distancing from the US in a significant way. Despite these efforts to deflect, increasing awareness of the human and economic costs of its delayed response further undermines the Trump administration's position, particularly as fatalities continue to mount and the Federal Reserve Board's chairman foresees a very slow return to economic normal through the end of 2021.

Looking back, China's central government strict enforcement of lockdown in Wuhan, which went as far as to lock people in their homes, and its use of technology to trace the movements of contaminated individuals saved tens if not hundreds of thousands of lives. While China can be criticized for its containment methods and should have been more transparent throughout the process, the government's handling of the crisis domestically must be given high marks. Overall, it was comparatively a success. Nevertheless, China's GDP growth for 2020 remains uncertain as consumers favor savings over consumption until confidence is fully restored and exports to countries affected by the economic downturn return to normal.

Many countries, the US and China included, are racing to develop Covid-19 treatments and vaccines, and early results look promising. But uncertainty remains high and will likely remain so until testing, treatment and tracing regimens are further developed.

Since the original publication of this book in 2019, the US has increased its effort to bar Huawei's access to US advanced technology, especially nano-chips. Initially applied to US manufactured chips only, the ban now includes chips made anywhere in the world using American technology. Meanwhile, China is accelerating its efforts to reduce its dependency on American technology.

Should this trend lead to further decoupling, and ultimately different models and standards for the world's two largest economies, the global economy will suffer from the resulting inefficiencies. Many countries equipped with Huawei technology are already threatened by the US actions against the company.

The other unanswered question is the form of China's potential retaliation. While the US has dominated the global economy for centuries, China has become a huge and attractive market for foreign companies. If China restricts market access for major US companies, the US economy will suffer.

Finally, there are important new developments in Hong Kong. In response to the sustained demonstrations in Hong Kong, the Chinese government enacted mainland security measures in an effort to accelerate integration between Hong Kong and China. These actions are condemned by the US and many other Western democracies, which view them as an abuse of power. Despite this, and using sustained demonstrations in Hong Kong as justification, the Chinese government recently began arresting protest leaders and continues to crack down on demonstrations. Should this continue, which it likely will, the three core constituencies in Hong Kong – the democratic-leaning government, the people of Hong Kong and the business community – must ultimately decide what accommodations they are willing to make to create a sustainable economic and political model. The issues of personal freedom, lack of affordable housing and the impact of any change in the rule of law on international institutions based in Hong Kong must all be addressed. How different the new Hong Kong will be from what it is today is a huge unanswered question.

Taken together, the issues of trade, Covid-19, technology and Hong Kong drive increasing tensions between the US and China. The upcoming US presidential election will likely exacerbate the situation. The Trump administration may be the driving force behind current tensions, but both parties are likely to maintain the pressure, albeit in different ways. How the rest of the world will react is an important question. As more countries push back on the US's attempt to constrain Huawei, join China's Belt Road Initiative and resent the weaponization of the US dollar, globally the pendulum may be swinging in China's favour.

★ ★ ★

INTRODUCTION

★ ★ ★

*"Let China sleep,
for when she wakes,
she will shake the world."*

– Napoleon Bonaparte

My first connection to China was a spiritual journey over 35 years ago. I wanted to identify with and learn from the lives of individuals who 'died with a smile'. That journey took me east, to Taoism and the Tao Te Ching written by Lao-tzu in the 6th century BC.

Since then I have taken over 80 trips to China, connecting with hundreds of individuals: Chinese business executives and managers, regulators and other governmental officials, experts in a wide range of social and economic fields, and many individuals interested in Taoism.

I gained a very positive impression of China through three and a half decades of relationships and interactions. I witnessed highly competent and educated executives and government officials, happy and optimistic people with a high level of pride in what China has accomplished, a high level of confidence in the central government, a profound awareness of China's history and culture, and a strong commitment to family, the future of China and its people.

Over the last 25 years I have read extensively on Chinese history, philosophy and literature, including many books on China written by Western authors. I also closely followed articles and editorials written in the Western press, specifically *The New York Times, Financial Times, The Wall Street Journal* and *The Economist*. While I believe some writers deeply understand China, Thomas Friedman, Henry Kissinger and Hank Paulson for example, the larger, emerging picture of China based on my readings is very different from my personal experiences.

The readings suggest an authoritarian and harsh Chinese government oppressing an unhappy population that experiences a total absence of human rights. They speak of China as a heavy polluter indifferent to the environment, an economy thriving thanks to unfair trade practices supported by an undervalued currency, a lack of innovation and the systematic theft of America's intellectual property. They fear a growing and aggressive military threat, the violation of the rights of the people of Taiwan and

Hong Kong and suppression of minorities in Tibet and Xinjiang. They draw unfair parallels between Communist China and the former Soviet Union, which was known for its aggressive military, and its failed and centrally managed economy, with leaders stealing the country's wealth at the expense of people.

I tried to dig into the root causes of this disconnect and this book presents my findings.

I should confess from the outset that this book represents a synthesis of my experiences and impressions in China and ideas from a wide range of sources. Original research is modest and the book focuses on the core story. To the best of my abilities, it is intended to be balanced, objective, logical and consistent with the basic facts.

My first step is understanding the fundamental characteristics and drivers of the US and Chinese governance, economies and social models. The first conclusion is they are very different on many core dimensions and that those differences are largely rooted in each country's history and culture.

The US model is best described as:

- Individualistic
- Ideological
- Dualistic: right/wrong, winners/losers
- Minimalist role of the government domestically
- Electoral democracy
- Economic model based on capitalistic free enterprise and open markets
- Absolutist approach to human rights
- Expansive view of global role spreading democracy and human rights

These characteristics reflect the will of the early settlers, who left Europe to escape limited economic opportunities available to lower socio-economic classes and the absence of human and religious rights. Since its founding, the US benefited from a relatively benign environment, with few foreign threats, safe borders and abundant natural resources.

The Chinese model is best described as:

- Strong central government run today by the Chinese Communist Party
- Consensus-driven and efficient decision-making similar to a corporate governance model
- A democracy, defined as a government 'responsive to the people'
- Leaders selected through meritocracy, not by popular election (except at the local level)
- Collective, with the family and society's wellbeing of far greater importance than the individual's
- Relativist rather than absolutist approach to human rights
- Highly pragmatic versus ideological mindset – focus on consequences rather than a 'right or wrong'
- Modest but growing global aspirations driven by economic self-interest and territorial integrity, as opposed to spreading the Chinese model

To develop a deeper understanding of these differences, this book explores a number of core drivers and their implications. The overall conclusion is that the major driver of misunderstanding is the US's judgement of China through Western eyes, without regard for the role China's history and culture play in shaping who China is today. As an illustration of the magnitude of the two different views of China, I have included two quotations from David Shambaugh's book, *China Goes Global*. From the author: "This suggests to me that it is not so much an aggressive or threatening China with which the world should be concerned, but rather an insecure, confused, frustrated, angry, dissatisfied, selfish, truculent, and lonely power." Whereas Vice Foreign Minister Fu Ying has a different take on the issue: "We don't view ourselves as a superpower.

You are not going to see a US or Soviet Union in China. You are going to see a culturally nourished country with a big population, being more content, being happy, being purposeful – and it will be a friend to the world. There is no reason to worry about China."

The objective of the book is to promote mutual understanding by the US and China through the explaining of each country's model and the evolution of each country's unique culture and history. For Americans, a fresh look at China should address how and why the country has evolved the way it has over its 4,000 years, which goes far beyond the brief 70 years of the Chinese Communist Party's leadership. Conversely, Chinese should appreciate the role of America's split from Europe and the early decisions of the Founding Fathers in the shaping of modern day America. In neither case does the book suggest that core changes in either country's model is likely, much less advisable. Beyond the models, the book compares and contrasts the evolution of each country's economy, education systems, human rights record, definition of democracy, worldview and military role. The book concludes with a call for constructive engagement on a range of non-combative global issues that would benefit enormously from cooperation between the US and China.

The book covers:

1. Context: what elements of the governance models and mindsets are grounded in history and culture and will not change
2. Culture: core source of differences
3. Economic performance: the true battlefield
4. Education systems: increasingly important, given the growing role of advanced technologies
5. Human rights and the rule of law: the US's absolutist ideology vs. China's relativist approach
6. Forms of democracy: the US's electoral compared to China's 'responsive to the people'
7. Worldview and the military: the US focus on 'spreading democracy and human rights' vs. China's attention to its economic interests, not spreading a model
8. Where we go from here

CHAPTER
1

CONTEXT: ELEMENTS OF THE GOVERNANCE MODELS AND MINDSETS GROUNDED IN HISTORY AND CULTURE WILL NOT CHANGE

"The histories and cultures of countries are vastly different, so it is unrealistic to expect China to have a political system that parallels any other."

– Hank Greenberg, CEO of CV Starr and longtime CEO of AIG, with over 40 years of experience in China (from *The China Fantasy* by James Mann)

In the US, the prevailing story of China's growing economy and rising standard of living will inevitably result in popular demand for more human rights (freedom of speech, the press, religion, etc.). In this story, China's government is eventually forced to democratize by the increasingly well-off Chinese middle class, thanks to dramatic annual GDP growth over the past 40 years.[1] In China, the US is seen as an increasingly divided country run by a government unable to overcome its polarization, increasingly isolationist, and lacking in financial disciplines, as evidenced by soaring deficits and the 2008 financial crisis.

While the US President Donald Trump and China's President Xi Jinping have their own leadership styles, it should be emphasized that we are not comparing these two leaders, regardless of how influential or big their personalities are. We are discussing existing worldviews and political systems which are hardly new, are widely embraced, and are responsible for most of the negative impressions between these two countries. What both of these views miss is a fundamental grounding in the history and culture of each country. These fundamentals shaped the two models over the course of centuries leading up to today, and will continue to shape them going forward. Additionally, both models are, and have been, incredibly successful in meeting primary goals.

There are certain core issues on each side which are multidimensional and continue to evolve; these are addressed later. This chapter cites key characteristics of both models that are unlikely to change for the foreseeable future.

★ ★ ★

CHINA WILL REMAIN A STRONG, SINGLE-PARTY GOVERNMENT WITH UNLIMITED SCOPE

★ ★ ★

China's governance model is grounded in a history of strong, single-party or dynastic, central government driven by collectivist thinking and behaviour.

Historically, collectivism in China developed through two separate forces. The first was the necessity to unite collectively to protect and recover from natural disasters, like famine, flooding and raids by the nomadic armies of the north. The second was the teachings of Confucius in the 6th century BC, which outlined moral codes emphasizing the family unit and greater society as taking precedence over individuals. The individual's role isn't prominent and focuses on self-improvement through education, to better support the family and society. While the influence of Confucian values ebbs and flows through the centuries, depending on the ruling dynasty or government, its focus on family and society is firmly established in the Chinese culture. This collectivistic spirit led to a strong central government built to deliver two things: prosperity and stability. Prosperity is clear to see in modern day China, but stability is something that eluded the country following the Opium Wars, all the way through the Tiananmen Square riots. China has remained remarkably stable for the past 30 years.

The two Opium Wars, largely with Great Britain, took place from 1839 to 1860. Great Britain leveraged its superior naval power to enforce the opium trade in China over the objections of the Qing Dynasty. As a result of these wars, millions of Chinese became addicts, Hong Kong was ceded to Great Britain, over 80 ports were opened to foreigners, as was travel of foreigners to China. The first Opium War marked the beginning of China's subjugation by foreigners and what is known as China's Century of Humiliation, which is taught extensively in Chinese schools. The end of Chinese subjugation by foreigners came with the defeat of the Japanese in World War II. Later, violence shook China from the Civil War, ending in 1949 to the Tiananmen Square riots in 1989. These riots were triggered by the funeral of a former leader popular with students and stripped of power, as well as a surge in inflation and corruption tied to the lifting of price controls and hoarding. The tension escalated and Chinese troops were brought in, resulting in extensive violence and around 1,000 civilian deaths.

The Qing Dynasty, overthrown in 1911, was the last dynasty in China. Advancement during dynastic rule relied on nepotism and relationships, as well as the Imperial Examination System, which existed for 1,300 years. While this specific examination system ceased in 1905, China's National Civil Servants Examination and interviews are still very much used today in all entry-level government appointments and advancements. Major dynasties typically lasted two to three hundred years and lost power when they lost popular support. Loss of support came from a combination of a declining economy, oppressive taxes, corruption, famine and invaders. Regardless of the ruling power, the core elements of a strong central governing body remained unchanged through history with few exceptions. Since Mao Zedong took over following the Civil War, the core model has remained fundamentally unchanged. The only exception is that senior government officials are selected based on an organized meritocratic model, including examinations and interviews, not nepotism.

The durability of the Chinese Communist Party for the past 40 years, starting with the Reform and Opening Up period under Deng Xiaoping, is driven by its ability to deliver prosperity and stability to the people. With extreme poverty now drastically reduced, down over 85% in the last 35 years,[2] President Xi Jinping's third goal is restoring China to *a*, not *the*, leading position globally. By any measure, against these three core goals, the Chinese government delivers exceptionally well. It has the highest average GDP growth rate over 40 years among all major countries,[3] brought 850 million people above the international poverty line,[4] and positioned China's economy as the second largest in the world. All this happened with little to no international military action. Additionally, according to a 2017 Pew Research survey, the Chinese government has one of the highest levels of both popular support for the direction

of the country (83%) and people who believe their lives will be better in five years (76%) of any major country.[5]

So why has the West, especially the US, expected China to shift
from its single-party, central government to an electoral democracy? At the most fundamental level, Americans believe an electoral democracy is the only true form of governance 'by and of the
people', and therefore the only form of legitimate government. As
Winston Churchill famously said, "Democracy is the worst form of
government, except for all the others." A second ideological reason
to believe the Chinese model is not sustainable is that, without elections, there is no accountability. However, whenever lack of popular
support brought a turnover in the Chinese government historically,
it never brought about an electoral democracy. While new leadership emerged, the governance model remained unchanged.

Many point to the lack of human rights in China. In the US, human
rights were a key motivator behind the founding of the country and
the highest priority of the drafters of the Constitution and the Bill of
Rights, which declared those rights to be self-evident and inalienable.

Let us take a moment here to define the key differences between
a collectivistic country and an individualistic one. Individualistic
countries, like the US and much of the Western world, typically value
independence, self-reliance, competition, assertiveness, directness
and the promotion of self-interest. Collectivistic countries, like
China and much of Asia, value social interdependence, tradition,
cooperative and obedient behaviour, sensitivity and self-control.
These inherently different values are important to keep in mind
when discussing the differences between China and the US because
they are fundamental to understanding how both countries work,
as well as their relationship.

Human rights are a great example because they are, by their
nature, individual rights. The Chinese trade off the benefits of
individual rights against the impact they might have on society.
Two examples include the individual's right to bear arms, which
has deadly consequences in the US, and the freedom of the press,

which is directly controlled by the government in China and has free rein in the US.

There is no strong, visible public outcry for more individual rights in China. This is because the collective society is performing very well, justifying the slow but steady rate of expansion of personal freedoms to individuals. We must acknowledge, however, that if there is an outcry for expanded rights, it would likely be censored and we would not hear of it. Originally, the Chinese hukou system allowed the government to determine where individuals lived, worked, and whether or not they could travel. Today this system is largely gone, leaving these personal decisions in the hands of individuals, with the exception of determining access to public services. This includes education, healthcare and housing, and is particularly important for migrants.

Restrictions on political freedoms, on the other hand, have become tougher, with increased levels of press and internet censorship as well as strong crackdowns on dissidents and human rights lawyers. Any strong political dissonance, including large assemblies and actions deemed as 'undermining the effectiveness of the government', is not permitted and is punishable. While this issue creates a strong backlash in the US, it does not within the Chinese population. As long as the overall level of prosperity continues to grow, government approval is likely to remain high, despite limits on political freedom. While the US may reject this mindset (it does go against the very nature of the US model), it is widely shared in China.

This strong, collectivist mindset, cultivated over 4,000 years of Chinese history, supports the existence of today's strong, central government that follows tradition and puts China first. As long as this government continues to deliver for society at large, Chinese individuals are likely to be supportive. That being said, Chinese people's interest in more expansive political freedoms may increase as they become accustomed to higher levels of individual prosperity. There is some degree of backlash in major cities in China, commonly taking place on social platforms like Wechat and Weibo.

★ ★ ★

THE US WILL REMAIN AN ELECTORAL DEMOCRACY

★ ★ ★

The US governance model was created by individuals who left Europe for two primary reasons. The first was economic opportunities, which were, by and large, limited to the upper class. The second was limited human and religious rights. As eloquently described in Alexis de Tocqueville's classic, *Democracy in America*, colonists wanted a government "by and for the people" that offered maximum economic and personal freedoms. This is the model and value system that prevails today.

At the highest level the US government is designed to be 'minimalist', with the country's future powered by a robust capitalistic private enterprise economy that takes advantage of Americans' ambition, work ethic and ingenuity. While many Americans are frustrated by the inaction and dysfunctional behaviour of their federal government, few are aware that the 'minimalist' model, as described by Tocqueville, was a clear, purposeful choice made by the Founding Fathers. Like many, prior to research my instinct was to blame inept politicians rather than the model itself. The minimalist role is baked into the government's core design on four dimensions.

The first is a clear balance of powers across the executive, legislative and judicial branches of the government. While the executive branch has extensive powers in foreign affairs, its ability to make fundamental changes domestically is seriously restrained by the other two branches. The second constraint is an essentially adversarial, two-party system that generally can only enact major legislation when a single party controls both the executive and legislative branches. The third is national elections every four years ,with a maximum of eight years in power for one president, so an unpopular administration could be removed. Finally, the federal government's powers are specifically outlined, with all other powers and decisions devolving to state and local governments.

This government system relies on short terms in office and the distribution of power, the opposite of the governance model in China. For all of the reasons the strong, single-party government in China reflects the culture, history and values of the Chinese people, the American two-party, electoral democracy reflects its own culture, history and values.

Americans have, and likely always will, put the ideals of political freedom, personal freedoms, a private enterprise-driven economy and the pursuit of the 'American Dream' above all else. The federal government is designed to protect American interests, provide core services, provide oversight over the economy and manage the US relationship with the global community. It is also meant to delegate significant power and decision-making to individual state governments. However, neither the federal nor the state government is designed to be able to impose its will on any individual's life so long as that person is within the boundaries of the law. If the law is considered to be unfair in any specific case, the system provides the room and ability for any individual to fight or change those laws, beginning at the local level and progressing all the way up to the Supreme Court. This is the nature of the individualistic mindset.

While this model is not always practical, rational or effective, its core design and functions have remained consistent since the founding of the US. In that time, just shy of 250 years, this model helped create and maintain the strongest country and economy on the planet. To change it would require changing the core principles upon which the US was founded, meaning it's highly unlikely to happen.

★ ★ ★

CHINESE PEOPLE DO NOT PUBLICLY ELECT SENIOR GOVERNMENT OFFICIALS; INSTEAD THEY WILL CONTINUE TO BE ADVANCED THROUGH AN INTERNAL MERITOCRATIC PROCESS

★ ★ ★

Because China is not an electoral democracy, some in the West believe it operates under some form of dictatorship. This is rein-forced in Bruce Dickson's recent book, *The Dictator's Dilemma*. It is also untrue. China's government functions as a sophisticated meritocracy that is powered by consensus decision-making.

It starts by encouraging bright young people to enter government service, something the US doesn't do. This 1,300-year-old model is grounded in a nationwide examination system offering enrollment in the country's best universities to the top performers. While the Imperial Examination System ended in 1905, the idea that the highest calling is government service largely remains, despite the recent call for top talent to go into business as well.

China's recent push for top talent to also focus on business is, ironically, commonplace in the US. Because of the strength of the business sector in the US, there are more economic and personal incentives for individuals to enter business rather than pursue a career in politics. Whether this begins to happen in China as the economy continues to grow and prosper is yet to be seen.

Once in the Chinese government, the performance and career paths of the top several thousand in ministries, the Chinese Communist Party, state-owned enterprises, major cities and provincial governments are all managed by the Organization Deparment of the Party. After an individual is nominated and elected to the National People's Congress, just shy of 3,000 individuals, he or she is eligible to be elected to the core governing body: the Central Committee of roughly 200. Advancement is subject to both a performance assessment of the Organization Department and their peers' assessment by individual judgment and teamwork. A similar process leads to advancement from the Central Committee to the Politburo of 25, and to the highest-ranking body: the Standing Committee of seven. While advancement in this model is not by popular election, the process is rigorous, ensuring that individuals have strong performance records over a wide range of positions and the respect of peers.

This model is most similar to the one used by major global corporations to select leaders for key positions.

While many question the accountability of the Chinese system, the turnover rate of the Central Committee is 60% every five years, which far exceeds turnover in the US Congress.[6] This suggests a relatively high degree of accountability within the system, even though we are unable to see it. There is also a significant amount of rotation incorporated into promotional systems within the Chinese government, which helps avoid entrenchment at the most senior levels. Though some degree of advancement realistically is corrupt and relies on relationships, this high turnover ensures the effectiveness of the overall system.

The natural popular appeal of the electoral democracy model of 'one man, one vote' is understandable. In theory, elected officials deliver or they are voted out. In reality, there are compromises with this system as there are with any other. These include a reliance on voter turnout, adversarial parties, campaign financing, uneven voting laws, a 'winner takes all model' that doesn't always reflect popular opinion, and difficulty finding qualified, electable candidates. Despite all of these complications, this model still works in a country like the US because of its individualistic values and belief in an electoral democratic system.

This model does not, however, reflect the values inherent to China. While the complications within China's government are shielded from the public, the results it delivers are indisputable, as is the popular support it garners from its people. Because of this, it's highly unlikely, downright impossible some might say, that China will switch to some form of an electoral democracy for positions above local governance.

THE WORLDVIEWS OF THE US AND CHINA ARE FIRMLY ESTABLISHED AND WILL NOT FUNDAMENTALLY CHANGE. THE US IS INCLINED TO BE POLITICALLY INTERVENTIONIST. CHINA WILL BECOME MORE GLOBAL, BUT ONLY TO ADVANCE ITS ECONOMIC INTEREST

Starting with the Monroe Doctrine in 1823, when President James Monroe declared that any foreign colonization or intervention in the Western Hemisphere required US approval, through to the most recent War on Terror, the US holds a global position for attempting to expand democracy, promoting human rights and taking initiatives against threats to US interests. Under President Trump, the US began sending signals that it is considering pulling back from historic commitments overseas. In the face of nearly 200 years of proactive global involvement, it's now uncertain as to how the US global role evolves going forward.

China, on the other hand, is historically an internally focused country, focusing on the wellbeing of the country, with foreign affairs limited to economic dealings and protecting China's territory and 'face'. Thus far, China expresses no real interest in influencing the governance models of other countries. The much discussed 'soft power' employed by China, especially in developing countries, better positions China for economic, not political, gain.

That being said, China is currently assembling the strongest navy in its history. While assertive in regards to its self-declared rights in the China Seas, its military budget remains modest, about one third of the US budget, and remains positioned as largely defensive. China's record of foreign military aggression over the past 1,000 years, one excursion into Korea and two into Vietnam, ranks at the low end of all developed countries, and this seems unlikely to change. China, historically, is much more involved militarily within China, dealing with invasions, civil wars and rebellions, than anywhere outside of its modern borders.

Whether China is or is not interested in imposing its political or ideological influence, economic influence is another story. We will examine this in Chapter 3 when we discuss the economy.

★ ★ ★

CHINESE CHARACTERISTICS CREATE MISUNDERSTANDINGS IN THE US

★ ★ ★

After factoring in these four 'givens', the major source of misunderstanding between the US and China is the different mindsets and attitudes of Americans and Chinese. Arthur H. Smith, an American missionary who lived for many decades in China during the 19th century, wrote a book in 1894 entitled *Chinese Characteristics*. Lin Yutang also identified similar characteristics of the Chinese people in his classic, *My Country and My People*.

What is striking about the Chinese characteristics is how many of them overlap with those used to describe Americans, including ambition, work ethic, optimism, friendliness, helpfulness and a sense of humour. But a number of other Chinese characteristics are not shared by Americans and create misunderstandings and tensions.

The first characteristic far more significant in China than America is 'face', which can be understood as someone's reputation or level of prestige.[7] An individual's face is a sum of their accomplishments, which then instructs how much respect they are due by others. Failing to show someone the proper amount of face, whether purposeful or accidental, can make a relationship uncomfortable and unproductive. This can mean anything from tactlessly discussing past failed efforts to seating someone at the wrong seat at a conference room table. However, these customs are mostly unspoken, making them hard to navigate for foreigners who are unused to the necessity of face in all levels of relationships. Americans are far more inclined to appreciate directness and disapprove of what they perceive to be ostentation or a time-wasting custom.

Face also plays an important role in the emerging trade war between the US and China. The US initiated significant tariffs on Chinese goods and, according to the administration's top trade advisor, Peter Navarro, no country would dare to retaliate. The US could, with some justification, argue that tariffs were the best response to the Chinese' persistent theft of US intellectual property, focused on the high tech sector, which is becoming the key economic battleground between the two countries. Whether tariffs were an appropriate response to the issue is not the point. The primary point is that the US was surprised by the Chinese response of imposing tariffs on US goods. If the US understood the importance of face to the Chinese, their response would have been completely predictable. China's response also showed the Chinese people that its government would not back down from a US challenge.

Another core difference is how Americans and Chinese conceptualize time. In the US, 'time is money'. We value hard work, and a component of hard work in America is inevitably the speed at which it is carried out. When commitments are made we immediately rely on timelines and deadlines to track progress and efficiency. Many traditional Chinese businesses, and the Chinese government, are interested in slow and steady progress and long-term efficiency over immediate timelines or deadlines. In short, they take the long view, a mindset grounded in ancient Taoist principles emphasizing 'going with the flow'.

There is also the issue of communication style. Americans pride themselves on being direct. The Chinese are indirect. Rather than giving direct answers, they tend to meander around a point with observations, feeling and inclinations, with a high level of vagueness. Some of this approach is buying time to make sure they are comfortable before committing and some is to avoid losing face if they need to reverse themselves. Dealing with this approach requires patience, something Americans don't always have. American frustration with countless meetings and discussions may feel legitimate, especially once 'time is money' is factored in. Americans might see this style of communication a waste of time, maybe even evasive. However, this emphasis on numerous, drawn-out discussions is vital for the Chinese when it comes to making important decisions and connections. These opposite styles of communication can easily contribute to person-to-person misunderstandings between Americans and Chinese.

Finally, while Americans frequently deal with issues at an ideological or conceptual level, the Chinese are typically more literal. The assertion that 'we have an understanding or an agreement in principle' is something the Chinese will readily agree to, knowing that the devil is in the details. On contentious issues like intellectual property theft, the Chinese will acknowledge the importance of protecting intellectual property rights, but until very specific agreements and enforcement mechanisms with consequences are instituted, the Chinese will regard high-level understandings as just that. US emphasis on contract law and the legal process as we know it is in its infancy in China, where 'guanxi', a system of social connections and relationships influencing business dealings, is commonplace and deeply rooted in its history.

Apart from mindset differences, a major source of misunderstanding is at the level of trust and understanding of motives. If the Chinese believe the primary motivation of the US is to contain China to protect the US's global leadership role, a high level of cooperation will be very difficult to create. If the US believes the Chinese Communist Party's primary objective is to perpetuate its position of power rather than putting China first, it will be difficult to cooperate. Individuals who know both sides very well – Henry Kissinger, for example – see two powers with many opportunities for cooperation on global issues such as climate change, the refugee crisis, cyber security and healthcare, with competition becoming largely economic and cultural rather than militaristic in nature.

The primary point here is that the debate on the future of the relationship between the US and China is simplified if the US accepts China's historic and cultural reality, just as China accepts the US's: that China is not destined to become an electoral democracy, just as the US is not destined to develop a one-party system. Obviously, specific leaders shape direction and outcomes within these models, but expecting models to change fundamentally is not grounded in reality. The two countries, though both powerful and influential, are inherently different in ways that are not necessarily negative so long as they can reach a high level of communication and cooperation at all levels of government, as well as business-to-business and people-to-people.

In order to do this, China and the US, Chinese and Americans, need to explore and acknowledge the differences inherent between them, as well as the similarities. If this can happen, these two powers have the opportunity to influence the world at large in significant and positive ways. Reaching this level of understanding is what we explore in this book, by examining the culture and education systems, economies, human rights issues, democratic models, education systems and worldviews of both the US and China.

CHAPTER
2

CULTURE: A CORE SOURCE OF DIFFERENCES

"The central conservative truth is that it is culture, not politics, that determines the success of a society."

– Daniel Patrick Moynihan, former US Senator

During my interview with Zhao Qizheng, former deputy mayor of Shanghai, he urged me to explore the differences in culture between the two countries rather than focus entirely on the 'hard' dimensions of economics, human rights and worldview. At his urging, I read *Culture Matters* by Lawrence Harrison and Samual Huntington. This book identified culture as the foundation for country development and is responsible for most of a country's mindsets and behaviours.

When a country achieves sustained economic success, credit typically goes to factors like population, natural resources, natural protections from enemies and a political system capable of effectively mobilizing people. But, as former US Senator for NY Daniel Patrick Moynihan points out, there is a deeper, more profound explanation: culture is the key determinant.

What Moynihan says makes sense. Policy decisions are important, but what truly drives an economy involves the hundreds of millions of people who comprise the workforce in the US and China. China's state-managed economy and the US's free enterprise, capitalistic economy are both sustained by the mindsets and behaviours of its frontline people and their managers.

Culture shapes the mindsets, behaviours, values and motivations influencing a country's work ethic, ingenuity and teamwork, which then produces economic outcomes. A simple test of this hypothesis is to compare China's economic performance to that of other authoritarian regimes and the US's to all democratic regimes. The performance spread within each group of countries, authoritarian and democratic, is enormous, suggesting that the political model is not a key factor.

In this chapter, we explore the cultures of the US and China and how each developed historically.

★ ★ ★

CULTURE

★ ★ ★

As covered in Chapter 1, the American and Chinese people share a number of important characteristics: strong work ethic, ingenuity, ambition, optimism, thriftiness, helpfulness and humour. But there are several important differences. American ingenuity creates bold, transformational, industry-shaping ideas: the evolution of the telephone, mass-produced automobiles, electrical and nuclear power, motion pictures and television, the computer, search engines and the internet, to name a few. Going back centuries, Chinese transformational inventions include gunpowder, the printing press, the compass, paper and silk.

More recently, Chinese inventions have been market-driven applications, frequently anchored in big, industry-shaping ideas developed in the US. Both bold inventions and market-driven applications are powerful economically, but they are fundamentally different. The iPhone, Facebook and Google's search engine are huge but monolithic inventions with well-defined features for the mass market. The Chinese use these mass-market creations to develop thousands of tailored applications uniquely suited to many different customer segments. These separate approaches to innovation enable both countries to remain leaders in the high-value-added technology businesses, including AI, 5G networks, robotics, advanced materials and biotech, which will dominate the global economy for decades. Though the US had a head start, China's ready access to US and foreign intellectual property allowed it to close the gap relatively quickly. Though each country's path is different, both demonstrate a high level of ingenuity sustained over a long period of time.

One key cultural difference between the US and China is reflected in hugely different savings rates. Americans are typically drawn to instant gratification, which goes hand-in-hand with an aggressive consumer market and a historically steady increase in living standards. This results in a savings rate of close to zero. The Chinese are more inclined to Confucian deferred gratification, evidenced by an average 35-40% savings rate. China's savings rate also reflects a far weaker social safety net, for both healthcare and retirement, than exists in the US.

Another key difference is overall mindset and values. America's are grounded in the pioneer spirit responsible for transforming the wilds of North America into the modern day US and the strongest economy the world has ever seen. This pioneer spirit is characterized by a can-do attitude, self-reliance, ambition and optimism, all reinforced by the sustained prosperity that followed.

Much of China's cultural mindset and values are grounded in Confucianism, which dates back to the 6th century BC and has played a shaping role in China's civilization ever since. As covered in the previous chapter, the core Confucian values are collectivistic, centrally focused on the family first and society second, with the individual's focus being on self-improvement through education, and the importance of harmony, respect and modesty.

★ ★ ★

CULTURE IN THE UNITED STATES

★ ★ ★

Culture in the US derives from the work ethic, ambition and optimism of the early settlers and the ingenuity that characterized its industrial revolution, turning the US economy into the world's strongest. From the 1870s to today, the US has become the land of opportunity, drawing tens of millions to immigrate to the US in the 19th and 20th centuries. Much of the economic success in the later half of the 20th and the early 21st centuries occurred through American advances in technology, which dramatically increased productivity and the standard of living. While economic success continues, income inequality and growing cultural differences between the liberal coasts and conservative heartland contribute to a high level of partisanship and threaten the country politically and socially.

The American culture developed over four broad and significant eras.

1. THE EARLY SETTLERS OF NORTH AMERICA EMBODIED AMBITION, COURAGE, OPTIMISM AND A STRONG WORK ETHIC

The early European immigrants demonstrated courage and self-determination by leaving all they had behind for the dangerous voyage and the unknown of the new world. They faced and overcame tremendous challenges, beginning with providing for their families while facing ongoing hostilities with the Native American Indians as well as British colonial oppression. Once established, they overcame a far superior British army and united the 13 colonies under the US Constitution.

The three core themes emerging from the Constitution were equal economic opportunity, maximum human rights and minimalist government. The challenge of getting all of the colonies on the same page created tensions that persist to this day in the adversarial two-party system. The first was the debate between the Federalists, seeking a strong central government, and the Democrats, who advocated for strong state rights. The second was between the North and the South on slavery, an issue only partially resolved by the Civil War, and subsequently with the Civil Rights Movement and the enforcement of anti-discrimination laws.

Once the country was firmly established, the next major development was the push westward to the Pacific and the establishment of, essentially, today's national borders. The core cultural themes emerging from this period included individualism, personal freedoms, ambition and optimism as the country became a major global power. The cultural dimension of ingenuity came to the forefront in the next strategic era.

2. THE INDUSTRIAL REVOLUTION, CHARACTERIZED BY INGENUITY AND WORK ETHIC, MARKED THE US ASCENSION TO GLOBAL ECONOMIC LEADERSHIP

Visionary inventors and scientists powered America, creating industry-shaping technologies that drove the American economy well into the 20th century and beyond. The intercontinental railroad, telephone and telegraph, electric power, mass-produced automobiles and revolutionary developments in farming equipment drove major advances in communication, travel and productivity. In the span of 60 years, the US went from being one of several strong economies to being the strongest globally and at the forefront of industrialization.

The cornerstone of this period was the ingenuity of American scientists, many of whom recently immigrated from Europe. Their work created global leading corporations like General Electric, US Steel, Ford Motor, General Motors and IBM. The leaders of industry displayed the creativity, ambition and critical thinking pioneered in US universities, graduate schools and research labs. Early industrial successes led to many others in healthcare, like Johnson & Johnson, and consumer products like Coca-Cola and Procter & Gamble, as well as retailers, like Sears and Walmart.

More recently, the US produced global leaders in advanced technologies: Apple, Amazon, Google, Facebook and Microsoft. American ingenuity, frequently driven by individual pioneers who possess the necessary vision, drive and access to open capital markets, clearly emerged over the past century as a cultural trademark of the American economy.

3. WAVES OF IMMIGRANTS, LARGELY IN THE 19TH AND 20TH CENTURIES, TURN THE US INTO A CULTURAL MELTING POT

Immigrants, initially from Europe and more recently from South America and Asia, face many similar challenges the early colonists faced. They leave their home country behind in search of opportunities and personal freedoms in the US. America's openness to immigrants reinforced its cultural heritage of equal opportunity and personal freedoms for all. Immigrants played a critical role in growing the US workforce and providing labour pools for jobs that American workers were reluctant to do. Many immigrants are also entrepreneurs, establishing small businesses in ethnic communities, some ultimately expanding to multiple US geographic regions, and some becoming major global corporations.

The US also has a large illegal immigrant population, estimated to be over 11 million people, at the heart of the polarization issue discussed in the next section. The anti-immigration movement wishes to shrink, or even eliminate, immigration on the grounds that immigrants take American jobs and have a higher proportion of criminals than the larger US population. On the former point, the facts suggest that the real challenge is the steady decline in manufacturing jobs, which is a global phenomenon attributable to advanced technologies such as robotics, artificial intelligence and, in the future, self-driving vehicles. On the latter point, facts show that illegal immigrants have lower crime rates than US citizens on average, which makes sense given the natural inclination an illegal immigrant has to avoid the law at all costs.

One important cultural difference between the US and China is the levels of multicultural immigration. Minority populations historically bring cultural heritage and customs with them when they immigrate to the US. This creates a multicultural America with less clarity on what defines 'American' culture today. China is a sharp contrast, with a dominant Han population accounting for 93% of all Chinese citizens. Additionally, the Han influence encroaches into minority regions like Tibet, Xinjiang, Inner Mongolia and others, as Han Chinese are encouraged by the government to resettle into those areas and are more likely to be appointed to the positions of power available there. The final picture shows China, with its long history of Confucianism and its dominant Han population, as a classic civilization state, while the US is more of a multicultural nation state.

4. MORE RECENTLY, THE US IS CHARACTERIZED BY A GROWING LEVEL OF POLARIZATION

The US is a dualistic Western society with 'winners and losers', polarized political parties, and different segments of society expecting and desiring different things. The most historically significant division was between the slave-owning states in the South and the anti-slavery states in the North. The tension began with the importing of slaves from Africa in the 17th century and grew until the North prevailed over the South in the Civil War, ending in 1865. Tensions on this topic continued through 1965, when legislation was passed to prohibit discrimination against African Americans in voting, housing, employment and education.

Slavery was not the only polarizing issue. During the development of the Constitution in the 1780s, two competing camps emerged: the Federalists, committed to a strong, central government, not unlike the monarchy in the UK, and the Democrats, interested in maximum state rights. This tension has persisted throughout US history, though the names of the parties changed. Recently, the Democratic Party favours a greater role for the Federal government on a wide range of social and economic issues. The Republican Party favours a smaller role for government and more freedom for the free enterprise economic model through lower taxes and fewer regulations.

While tensions and debates characterize the functioning of the government, the norm was for both sides to meet in the middle and compromise. This changed with the Supreme Court's Citizens United case, which ruled that political contributions were covered under the Constitution's right to free speech. This allows wealthy individuals and corporations to bypass restrictions on campaign contributions and make substantial contributions to support their views. Those views are typically extreme, and are reinforced by funneling powerful legislative committee assignments to politicians who support these views. Two examples of this are relaxed environmental regulation for large energy companies and a lack of meaningful regulation of the sale of firearms, something widely supported by the US population.

The result is the shrinking of moderate representatives and growth of the number of extremists in the US government. This phenomenon leads most senators and representatives to vote the party line and for the party in power to freeze out the opposing party from legislative deliberations. According to David Boren, a former US senator and author of *A Letter to America*, 83% of Americans don't believe the two political parties can come together to solve the country's problems.[1] Historically, the US always came together in times of crisis, whether it was military actions, environmental disasters, economic depressions or challenges like the Soviet Union's launch of Sputnik, the first satellite in space. Whether a crisis could be as unifying today is unclear.

Apart from political polarization, the US is divided on a socio-economic basis. Income inequality increased dramatically and is exacerbated by the 'middle class' tax cut, which will deliver 83% of the $1.5 trillion in benefits to the wealthiest Americans by 2027.[2] Another important factor is the steady decline in lower-middle income jobs for Americans who didn't attend college.

While some politicians point to immigrants and imports as the cause of the erosion of manufacturing and hourly rate jobs, the real reason is automation, lower cost overseas labour and companies using robots to replace many of these jobs. This trend will worsen as AI and self-driving vehicles replace a massive number of US jobs. This wealth split pits wealthier Americans, living predominantly in urban and suburban areas, against the economically depressed, who populate rural areas. Apart from the statistics, the hard reality many Americans are waking up to is this: the taken for granted expectation that everyone's standard of living will exceed their parents' is no longer true for many. In short, the American Dream is no longer a reality. This discovery is leading many Americans to look for someone to blame, and politicians capitalize on this anger by agreeing and promising a fix, though many of them ('no more immigration' for example) offer only the illusion of a solution.

Are the cultural challenges driving US divisiveness solvable? In theory, they are. Excessive tax benefits for the wealthy could be redirected to provide a livable wage for many. They could also provide many individuals more protection against major medical expenses. Investing in infrastructure and in the jobs of the future would benefit all. Apart from tax reform, avoiding the enormous cost of foreign wars (over $10 trillion on an inflation adjusted basis from the Vietnam War through the current War on Terror) could be redirected to tackling the social issues driving polarization.[3]

The core characteristics that enabled America to flourish (work ethic, ingenuity, high ambition) are still present. Whether the political system steps up for the common good or a crisis drives people to unite is an unanswered question. Given history, the question is not whether the US will rally, but when and how.

★ ★ ★

CULTURE
IN CHINA

★ ★ ★

While many roots of Chinese culture go back 4,000-plus years, the essence is embodied in the teachings of Confucius, who lived in the 6th century BC. The core components of his teachings were the family unit as the core building block of society, clear roles and responsibilities within the family, support and respect for society and the government, individual improvement through education, and the importance of respect and modesty. The overarching theme is harmony and balance.

The essence of Confucianism is fundamentally different from Western and American culture on two dimensions. The first is, as a collective culture, the family and society take precedence over the individual, whereas in the West the individual is pre-eminent. The second is that the Chinese culture focuses on compromise, not dualistic values. A lack of appreciation for these two core differences is at the heart of the mistrust and misunderstanding between China and the US today.

Before exploring how Confucianism endured for thousands of years as the cornerstone of Chinese culture, we should note that Confucius was a Chinese teacher, editor, politician and philosopher who lived from 551 BC to 479 BC. He focused solely on life on Earth as we know it. He left the cosmic questions (the source and evolution of life; the nature of the afterlife and who qualified) to the spiritualists who, in China, were predominantly Taoists and Buddhists.

The core beliefs and practices of Confucianism enduring for over 2,500 years, not only in China but in much of Asia, is remarkable and has few, if any, parallels. Its durability is explained by several factors. The first is its support by the ruling dynasties that embraced the discipline and order of Confucianism and benefited from the support and respect it claimed society owed the government. The second is that Confucius' teachings were anchored in China's education system and, in later years, the national examination system. Finally, his teachings are fully aligned with the core values of harmony and balance, which have long defined Asian values.

Let's explore the evolution of Confucianism through five eras.

1. THE HAN, TANG AND EARLY SONG DYNASTIES FULLY EMBRACED CONFUCIANISM

Confucianism was first broadly embraced by the Han dynasty. That dynasty was drawn to Confucianism's structure and discipline as a means to establish social order. This objective makes sense, following the violence of the Zhou Dynasty and the successful but brutal unification of China under the Qin emperor. The Han was the first, but hardly the only dynasty to adapt Confucianism to support its aspirations.

Another important spiritual and philosophic practice, Taoism, was popularized by Lao-Tzu roughly 2,500 years ago in China. The essence of Taoism is captured in the Tao Te Ching, or the 'Way of Life'. The core tenets of Taoism are: (1) life is an unknowable mystery exemplified by the wonders of nature; (2) life is made up of self-correcting and recurring rhythms and learning to go with these rhythms is key to fulfillment; (3) shedding attachments brings one closer to the Tao; and (4) by so doing one becomes a beneficial presence for all. Taoism is a spiritual philosophy and, with Buddhism and Confucianism, is one of the three philosophic and spiritual pillars of China. Among the three, Confucianism is more fully grounded in everyday life, focusing on the family, society, the role of the individual, education and governance, with an emphasis on harmony and moral balance.

The Tang dynasty embraced Taoism, but retained Confucianism as the heart of the education system and governance model. The early Song dynasty fully reinstated Confucianism and introduced an exam-based meritocratic approach for advancement to the most senior government positions. The decision to install a meritocracy, rather than a system based on class or birthright, is consistent with Confucian values and remained in place through the final dynasty, the Qing. The later Song dynasty introduced Neo-Confucianism, which increased its influence on the people through its focus on family.

Zhu Xi, the father of Neo-Confucianism, wrote *Family Rituals*, which became the practical guide for practicing Confucianism within the family. The goal was for everyone within the family to be virtuous and, ultimately, spread moral behaviour throughout society, not unlike the Christian 'do unto others as you would like them to do unto you'. This heightened focus on the family had great influence in Korea and Japan as well.

When the Mongols replaced the later Song dynasty, they concluded that China was too large and diverse for them to rule without a highly structured and disciplined model. So, much like the Han, they reinstituted Confucianism to establish order and control during the period of conquest. They also re-established the national examination system. Both the Ming and Qing dynasties espoused the core tenets of Confucianism: centrality of the family, moral governance, and meritocratic advancement of government officials through education and examinations. In practice, however, both dynasties were also plagued by corruption.

2. AFTER THE QING DYNASTY, CHINA'S SITUATION WAS CHAOTIC, MARKED BY WAR AND UNSTABLE GOVERNMENTS, LIMITING CONFUCIAN VALUES TO THE FAMILY

China's attempts to establish a republican government after the Qing dynasty failed and led to the rule of the warlords. The Kuo Min Tangl (KMT), also known as the Nationalists, and puppet governments run by Japanese eventually replaced the warlords. After the Japanese suffered defeat in World War II, a temporary truce between KMT and the Communists ended with a brutal civil war, as well as the Communists' eventual victory.

While none of the governments during this period embraced Confucianism, after 2,500 years the core theme at a local level, namely the family-first mentality and focus on education, provided an anchor for people terrorized by the unending wars and the lack of an effective government.

3. MAO TRIED TO WIPE OUT CONFUCIANISM INDIRECTLY WHEN HE FIRST TOOK OVER IN 1949 AND THEN OVERTLY DURING THE CULTURAL REVOLUTION

Mao sought to establish a new culture and recognized that Confucianism was deeply entrenched, meaning a new culture would only be possible with the eradication of the old. Ceremonies honouring Confucius were banned. During the Cultural Revolution, the 'four olds' (customs, habits, culture, thinking) were rooted out. The highly educated were the early targets and many were beaten to death. Families were scattered to different regions and forced to do manual labour. Mao's *Little Red Book* replaced Confucian writings. Confucius' grave at Qufu was disinterred as the final protest against his influence.

4. REVIVAL OF CONFUCIANISM UNDER DENG

Even the brutality of the Cultural Revolution could not eradicate the core tenets and values of Confucius. By then they were so baked into the culture that ten years of upheaval could not wipe out 2,500 years of practice.

After Mao, the Communists were confronted with this question: what could replace Marxism, which revolted against the inequality and suffering resulting from capitalism and focused on creating a classless society without personal property, as the regime's philosophical foundation? Deng and his successors found the answer in Confucius. Their revisiting of Confucian values found a perfect fit with the core themes of Deng's Reform and Opening Up: opposing ruthless oppression, and endorsing moderation and rationalism. Confucian emphasis on 'harmony' was fully embraced by the party. Confucian style meritocracy was also deployed by the Organization Department to advance officials based on their performance, potential, and peer respect and support.

Professor Li Zhou, after much study in the 1980s, concluded, "Confucianism is almost synonymous with Chinese culture."

5. BUT, MANY QUESTION SOME CONFUCIAN VALUES AND THE UNDERLYING MOTIVATIONS FOR THE CHINESE COMMUNIST PARTY'S EMBRACE OF CONFUCIANISM

Lin Yutang, author of bestsellers *My Country and My People* and *The Importance of Living*, objects to the negative consequences of Confucianism on many dimensions, but three stand out. The first is the overwhelming primacy of filial relationships. He says, "Confucius had eroded the dedication to community and nation that was so vital in the West by elevating the family too high." The second is the dominance of the father over the son. "By placing the son under the thumbs of their father, Confucius was preventing the emergence of a modern China." Lin's third objection was to the inherent subjugation of women in Confucian society, though he acknowledges that the treatment of women has improved significantly in China in terms of the freedom to decide whom to marry as well as where to live and to expand their role beyond the home to include employment.

On the issue of the underlying motivations of the party to embrace Confucianism, Michael Schuman in his comprehensive and thoughtful book, *Confucius and the World He Created*, expresses a somewhat cynical point of view. He says the Communists' "hope is that Confucius can help them preserve the status quo – and thus keep them firmly in power ... they are hiring Confucius as a public relations officer ... to use his image of wisdom and virtue to paint their own regime as benevolent and themselves as worthy, caring rulers."

★ ★ ★

LOOKING FORWARD

★ ★ ★

My exploration of the role of culture generated two insights. The first is that the power of Americans' work ethic, ambition and ingenuity has more than compensated for the historic differences in our political parties and has enabled the country to sustain global economic leadership despite the growing level of polarization in government.

For China, the attraction of Confucian values for dynasties and governments is understandable given the attraction to harmony, stability and respect for government that every regime aspires to. What is more surprising is that the core Confucian values continue to shape everyday life in China. The primacy of the family, the focus on education, and the values of self-improvement, respect and modesty are enduring values that survived over 2,500 years despite many periods of breakdown in governmental authority.

While the historical evolution of each country is reasonably clear, each faces meaningful uncertainties going forward.

1. Will the rising polarization in the US be reversed, leading to the return of moderates and compromise in Washington? Will this shift require a crisis to trigger the change? What are the likely consequences of ongoing polarization for the issues of income inequality, healthcare, education, infrastructure and national debt?

2. Will the younger Chinese population's accelerating exposure to prosperity undermine the core values of Confucianism: collective over individualistic, family first, deferred gratification and modesty?

CHAPTER
3

ECONOMIC PERFORMANCE: THE TRUE BATTLEFIELD

"The economy is the start
and end of everything.
You can't have successful
education reform or any other
reform if you don't have
a strong economy."

– David Cameron, former UK Prime Minister

Regardless of a country's specific economic model and ideology, economic performance is foundational to a country's economic health and key to winning the support of its people. Economic performance creates a sense of wellbeing and belief in a better future. At the most basic level, this means food on the table, housing, safety, health and a satisfying job. As those needs are met, it means meeting growing expectations. In this chapter, we explore the different models employed by the US and China, their core drivers, and how they've performed. We also examine the existing economic ties between the US and China and address the two economies' present issues.

Each economic model enables each country's aspirations. The US emphasizes prosperity, equal economic opportunity, personal freedoms, robust human rights, and the spread of democracy and human rights globally. China seeks prosperity, stability and returning to the global stage as a leading country and economy.

The economic models adopted by the US and China could not be more different and reflect each country's unique history and culture.

★ ★ ★

THE US
ECONOMIC MODEL

★ ★ ★

As described by Alexis de Tocqueville in his book *Democracy in America*, the US economic model promotes equal opportunity for all and performance-driven merit, rather than the class-driven model in Europe, where class decides opportunity. Under this model, the government's role is minimal and focused on enabling infrastructure, finance, trade, defense, foreign relations, rule of law and basic services. The economic engine is a capitalistic, free enterprise economy with competitive open markets, so essentially survival of the fittest. This model puts a premium on ingenuity, work ethic and open capital markets. By design, the best and the brightest are historically drawn to business, with its promise of wealth creation, family security, personal satisfaction and creative expression. In effect, the young country was counting on an organic, bottom-up model to drive its fortunes, with the government playing an enabling and regulatory, not shaping, role.

DRIVERS OF THE US ECONOMY

The US economy is driven by innovation and technology, a strong immigrant workforce, rich natural resources, a benign environment, a supportive government and, prior to China, major scale advances over economic competitors. Most of the drivers of the American economy are organic in nature, reflecting the bottoms-up nature of the economy.

1. INNOVATION AND TECHNOLOGY

The US has remained at the forefront of innovation and technology for the past 150 years, globally, and powered the global economy over this period. Groundbreaking inventions and innovations born in America include the telephone and telegraph, electric power, mass-produced automobiles, air travel, and semiconductors, leading to the more recent development of biotech, social media, artificial intelligence and the internet. The sources of many of these advances include corporate and university labs as well as government-sponsored research in aeronautics, space, nuclear energy and, most recently, the internet. European-born scientists, who immigrated to the US to escape war and the related oppression, are behind many discoveries and inventions. An education system promoting critical thinking was another key driver, giving the US the majority of truly breakthrough products and services over the past century. Finally, many influential technology companies began as startups funded by venture capital firms and supported by a robust capital market within the US.

2. A STRONG WORKFORCE POWERED BY IMMIGRATION

The US workforce is characterized by a strong work ethic, ingenuity and an effective education system. Immigration, initially from Europe and Asia and more recently from Latin America, played an important role. Those who managed to enter the US were motivated, in search of a better life, and responsible for the growth of the 20th century US economy, which would have been impossible without immigration. The 'America First' ideal and curbs on immigration are the antithesis of this historic strength. Outside of immigration, the dominance of US corporations in the global league tables also reflects the excellent US undergraduate and graduate school university system.

3. RICH NATURAL RESOURCES AND A BENIGN ENVIRONMENT

The US is blessed with rich natural resources in minerals and energy, plenty of arable land, a temperate climate and an abundance of natural ports and waterways for easy transportation. It is also separated from Asia and Europe on both sides by two oceans. Unlike Europe and Asia, which were torn by wars in the late 19th and 20th centuries, the US avoided any meaningful invasion since the Revolutionary War and experienced no major war on its soil since the Civil War. The loss of men of working age and property in Europe and Japan during the World Wars took a major toll on those countries' economies and ability to capitalize on an increasingly global economy.

4. A STRONG CONSUMER MARKET

The US consumer market is historically the most robust in the world. The high consumption rates are the counter of low savings rates, which historically reflected the strong optimism Americans are known for. Just three years ago, in 2016, the US ranked third in the world, after Switzerland and Norway, in household consumption expenditure per capita, at $36,373.[1] The hollowing out of the middle class and decline of manufacturing jobs now threaten this consumer-driven economy.

5. SUPPORT FROM STATE AND FEDERAL GOVERNMENTS

The federal government deals with all issues that cut across state lines, including finance issues, trade, interstate commerce and more. The states deal with issues wholly contained within the state. Although the federal and state governments' roles are modest in terms of influential innovations and technologies, they played an important supportive role on a number of dimensions: building the US highway system, rail lines, waterways and airports to support efficient transport of goods and services across the country; establishing strong anti-trust laws to prevent monopolistic practices; and providing a strong patent system to protect innovations and intellectual property. Finally, the development of the World Trade Organization (WTO) protects free trade, and the Treasury and Federal Reserve Bank manage the money supply and interest rates responsible for keeping inflation under control. The rapid rate of innovation and technological development would be impossible without these important government investments. While the influence of government is overall positive, there have been important lapses over time. While free trade is a win/win situation, specific unfavourable trade agreements led to disadvantages for the US and, ultimately, trade inequities. And, while intellectual property (IP) rights are protected under the law, prior to 2017 little was done to enforce them, enabling China and others to take advantage of US IP without a quid pro quo.

★ ★ ★

CHINA'S
ECONOMIC MODEL

★ ★ ★

The Chinese economic model is top-down and state managed. This top-down, centrist model is responsible for generations of successful Chinese history, making the Chinese economy the global leader for much of its history – up to as recently as 1820 – driven by its huge population and an agrarian economy. A social pecking order, attracting the best and brightest to be government officials, rather than business men and women, enabled the Chinese model. This model leaves government officials with control of the economy, ensuring that key economic levers (taxation, land use, investment, law, finance, trade) remain aligned. This historic model lapsed during the 19th and the majority of the 20th centuries due to the Opium Wars, the Taiping Rebellion, the first Japanese War, the collapse of the corrupt Qing dynasty, the warlord period, the second Japanese War, World War II, the Civil War and the disruptions under Mao. After Deng took over in 1978 and launched the Reform and Opening Up initiative, the Chinese economy came roaring back. Opening up enabled China to get access to advanced countries' technology and, by joining the WTO in 2001, global trading markets. Today we are seeing the effects of China's late industrial revolution, which was delayed by over 100 years as a result of foreign oppression, civil war and the Cultural Revolution under Mao.

The consequences of the Chinese industrial revolution are, ironically, identical to America's: corruption driven by rapid wealth creation, income inequality, exploitation of labour, pollution and intellectual property infringements. Much of the West's criticism of China over the past 40 years glosses over this point.

In China, the executive branch is in control, rather than a balance of power between judicial and legislative branches, and there is effectively a single-party system. Strong central control over the economy enables China to make rapid and bold strategic moves to upgrade the economy. While the US objects to the Chinese government subsidizing target industries, it's how China historically operates. Many in the US believe their government should consider doing the same to counter China.

Leaders under this single-party system are selected and advanced meritocratically, based on rigorous performance reviews carried out by the Organization Department of the party and election by peers. This process means most senior leaders boast a strong education background and experiences covering the ministries in Beijing, major city and provincial governments, state owned enterprises (SOEs) and the Chinese Communist Party. A rigorous rotation system ensures broad experiences.

China's economic model, while similar to a US corporation, is far more powerful on two dimensions. The first is control over all of the factors driving economic performance, including labour supply, tax policy, finance policy, trade agreements, laws and regulations, and agreements with other countries to access mineral and energy supplies. The second is the ability to tap in to the country's financial resources to make mega-investments generally incorporated in China's five-year plans, including next generation technologies and initiatives, such as the Belt and Road Initiative (BRI). These two levers, along with the corporate governance model, enable China to make and execute major strategic decisions quickly and efficiently. One example is China's shift from an agrarian economy to becoming the world's leading exporter of manufactured goods by leveraging low-cost labour. Deng also shifted the focus of the Chinese economy from SOEs to private companies, enabling the economy to become market driven. Finally, Deng's approach for China to keep a low profile globally enabled China to take advantage of Western technology and free trade with no meaningful pushback.

DRIVERS OF CHINA'S ECONOMY

China is first and foremost a state-guided economy. To many in the West, this conjures central planning driven by supply rather than market. For many Americans, this feels reminiscent of the centrally managed (and failed) Soviet economy. So what drove China's economic success over the past 40 years?

1. CORPORATE GOVERNANCE MODEL

One of Deng's first trips as leader was to Singapore, where he met the country's founder and leader, Lee Kuan Yew. Singapore became an economic miracle in a relatively short period of time due to its economic model, which is patterned on a major corporation: a strong leader/CEO, a board of directors to provide direction and oversight, strong management selected meritocratically, and a focus on both long-term strategic direction and short-term execution. Decisions are made through consensus and behind closed doors without external interference. Singapore holds elections, but the ruling party historically wins with a large margin. This model is not possible under a democratic governance model with adversarial parties, transparency and a balance of power across three branches of government.

Bold strategic decisions instituted by the government enabled China to sustain its strong economic growth over the past 40 years. Each of these decisions played a pivotal role in driving China's economy and would have been impossible without a strong central government to drive execution.

- The Household Responsibility System provided incentives to farmers to boost and diversify output by enabling them to sell on the open market whenever they produced in excess of their quota.[2]
- The creation of Township Village Enterprises (TVEs) in 1982 created a wave of entrepreneurial energy by lifting restrictions on where entrepreneurs could sell their products. Investment funds poured into small entrepreneurs from Hong Kong, Taiwan and overseas Chinese. These entrepreneurs leveraged new technologies from abroad and represented the first phase of China's manufacturing-for-export industry. Employment in these enterprises rose from 28 million

in 1978 to 135 million in 1996. Output rose from less than 6% of GDP to 26% during this same time period.[3]

- The creation of Special Economic Zones in Shenzhen and other coastal cities following Deng's Southern Tour in 1992. The economic incentives boosted the smaller scale successes of the TVEs and enabled China to become the world leader in manufacturing for export, capitalizing on low labour costs. These zones allowed for experimentation with different trading terms.

- Massive investment in infrastructure, averaging over 8% of GDP from 1992 to 2013, enabled China to build world-class highways, high-speed rail lines, ports, airports and cities quickly. The global average during this same time period was only 3.5% of GDP. The US invests approximately 2% of GDP in infrastructure annually.[4]

- The $1 trillion BRI initiative leverages infrastructure building capacity and trade with countries in Asia and developing countries. This initiative is not without controversy, given its vulnerability to corruption and the risk of developing countries taking on too much debt and sacrificing control over the projects.

- Looking forward, the 2025 Initiative in technology-intensive industries, if successful, will shift China's economy from lower-value-added manufacturing for export to high-value-added industries such as software, AI, biotech, advanced computers, robotics and aerospace.

2. URBANIZATION

Urbanization is a key engine of economic growth for China. As senior fellow in the Carnegie Asia Program, Yukon Huang pointed out in his book, *Cracking the China Conundrum*, that the productivity of a farmer increases by a factor of six when he relocates to an urban area.[6] Since his wages don't increase accordingly, the shift creates an economic surplus for the economy. As of 2017, China was 58% urbanized. According to the World Bank and McKinsey Global Institute analysis, Germany was 73% urbanized in 1979 and Japan was 78% in 1995.[7] This suggests that China's benefit from further urbanization would be substantial. The productivity lift from urbanization is huge and enables the government to more efficiently deliver public services – education, healthcare and housing – than in rural areas. The short-term challenge remains the funding of those services through the hukou system. Urbanization also comes with human challenges. These include the difficulty of getting public services for migrants and the pressures on the older generation remaining in rural areas with children. State-sponsored urbanization provides a good illustration of the difference in a collective society. Urbanization at the scale China has accomplished, and in the relatively short time frame, is impossible in an individualistic society. The reason urbanization happened at a naturally slower pace in countries like Japan, Korea and Western societies is that public services are available and economic incentives are strong for individuals who make the decision on their own.

3. A LARGE AND RAPIDLY GROWING MIDDLE CLASS

China's economy is increasingly fueled by consumer consumption, which accounted for nearly 80% of GDP growth in the first half of 2018.[8] Services play a critical role in driving consumption, accounting for 52% of GDP growth in 2017, up from 44% in 2010.[9] The upside in services growth is enormous given high restrictions on foreign-provided services, which are likely to free up over time. More importantly, the productivity of services in China is estimated to be between 15 and 30% the average of OECD countries.[10] The engines driving services growth are education and healthcare, the latter of which will see dramatic growth for years to come. In 2015, China spent only 5% of GDP on healthcare compared to the global average around 10%.[11] An indication of the scale of China's consumer market is the estimate that, by 2027, its growing middle class will surpass those of the US and EU combined.[12]

4. THE SHIFT FROM STATE-OWNED ENTERPRISES TO PRIVATE ENTERPRISE

When Deng took power in 1978, all major businesses in China were government- or military-owned. Working for an SOE was considered an 'iron rice bowl' job, where the government provided all basic needs of the worker from cradle to grave. Deng understood that the SOE model was inconsistent with improving productivity over time and driving performance, so the government set in motion a program to encourage the development of private enterprises and streamline or shut down unproductive SOEs. The 'iron rice bowl' model was replaced with a focus on performance and productivity, causing millions of layoffs. To avoid the social disruptions these layoffs could have caused, the timing was aligned with the takeoff of the manufacturing for export sector, which created millions of jobs. Finally, SOEs were opened to public ownership through minority share IPOs, further increasing the pressure to perform. This approach is in sharp contrast to what happened in Russia, where major SOEs were sold to oligarchs at suppressed prices, leading to the enrichment of a small number of owners at the expense of the country.

If we fast-forward to 2018, over 60% of the economy and 80% of urban employment is driven by the private sector, thanks to large companies like Ping An, Huawei, Alibaba and Tencent.[13] While the performance of SOEs is improving, the return on capital remained approximately half of the private sector just a decade ago.[14] A major contributor to the underperformance of SOEs is the lack of CEO control over critical personnel decisions affecting senior teams. Those decisions on assignments are made by senior party officials based on the recommendations of the Organization Department of the Party. This creates three fundamental problems:

- Executives are left in their position for three to five years, which leads them to focus on short-term performance at the expense of strategic investments in the future.

- I saw first-hand through my consulting role with Chinese SOEs that many roles are given to individuals lacking the industry and functional experience required for the role. While many are highly educated and talented, they cannot be effective if they lack relevant experience.

- The CEO is not empowered to drive the company if he or she retains little control over the senior team. Executives are more beholden to the Organization Department for their advancement than to the CEO, which leads them to make critical strategic and operating decisions the CEO may disagree with. This model also leads to cautious decision-making due to the belief that the downside of making a mistake is greater than the upside of making a good bet. This model is in sharp contrast to practices in the highly competitive private sector, where strong, visionary, founder CEOs keep total control over their teams and shape their company's future. Industry-shaping companies like China's Alibaba, Huawei, PingAn, Tencent and the US's Apple, Amazon, Facebook and Google could have never been built under the SOE model.

5. A HUGE CONSUMER SAVINGS RATE

China's consumer savings rate of 35–40% provides enormous funds for investment.[15] This is in sharp contrast with the US, which has an average consumer savings rate of close to 6% (1960-2018).[16] Some of this high rate is grounded in the thrifty nature of the Chinese and the Confucian value of deferred gratification. The rest is explained by the relatively underdeveloped safety net provided by the government. Chinese consumers must fund their own retirement income and save for healthcare in the event of serious illness and assisted living services. While the consumer savings rate is an important source of investments for the country, those savings are not used efficiently. The bulk of the funds are invested at very low rates of interest in state-owned banks, providing funding for the government and SOEs, which generate relatively low returns. Funneling those funds to private enterprises as investments or loans would give the economy an important lift.

6. ACCESS TO WESTERN TECHNOLOGIES AND MARKETS

China's economic success would have been slower without access to Western technology and markets. Deng recognized early in his tenure that economic gaps between China and Japan, Korea and the West were due to technology-driven productivity gaps. His trips to developed countries focused on getting access to technology and manufacturing expertise. The US was late to recognize China as an economic competitor and blind to the extent to which access to Western technology and favourable trade agreements have fueled China's rise. China's growing self-sufficiency in advanced technologies, with the notable exception of semiconductor manufacturing, and the declining importance of exports to its economic success suggests that the US's actions are too little, too late. Part of China's success in taking advantage of the West goes back to Deng's suggestion for China to quietly go about its business and keep a low profile. Beyond technology, China's entry into the WTO, with US clearance, provided access to global markets, fueling a sharp increase in China's exports. China's entry has also increased pressure from the US to open their markets as a quid pro quo.

7. ENTREPRENEURIAL CAPABILITIES

The Chinese people, at home and abroad, boast a long track record of entrepreneurialism. For many centuries, this energy focused on building small- and medium-sized businesses, from restaurants and cleaners to retail shops. The first major wave were the TVEs, launched by Deng in the 1980s. More recently, China is creating new businesses at scale that accounts for 91 unicorns (startups with a value of at least $1 billion). That represents close to 30% the number of unicorns globally.[17] Unlike the US, the leader in major breakthrough technologies for the past 250 years, China's startups are typically based on applications tied to US-driven breakthrough technologies.

While Apple, Google and Facebook created enormously successful products, they built fully integrated products consumers could choose to buy or not. China, with its enormous consumer market, looks at all possible applications of a monolithic product, sees the huge potential variations for different customer segments, and creates those specialized products. Even a sharply defined segment can be a multi-billion dollar segment in China. The expected explosion in AI creates enormous opportunities in China, with most experts saying China is equally advanced as the US in this area and is likely to develop even faster, given a fourfold advantage in population and far fewer privacy limitations compared to the West.

Many entrepreneurial opportunities will fuel the services sector, where China's productivity lags far behind that in OECD countries. Critical innovations are already occurring in payments, with WeChat and Alipay on the verge of making cash payments obsolete in China through scannables and bar-codes, which are used in nearly every establishment in large cities across China, as well as person-to-person.

8. THE ACCELERANT OF CORRUPTION

While corruption undermines the people's trust in the government, Yukon Huang points out in his excellent book, *Cracking the China Conundrum*, economic decisions involving SOEs, the private sector and government officials at every level are accelerated by bribes and other forms of corruption.[18] Without the grease of corruption, the government approval process takes far longer. While few support corruption as a matter of principal, its role in accelerating decision time frames is a reality.

9. COMPETITION AMONG PROVINCIAL GOVERNMENTS AND MAJOR CITIES

The central government encourages a high level of competition among provincial governments and major cities to foster economic growth in centrally determined directions. Leaders are evaluated based in part on economic metrics, which influence both incentives and promotions. The inherent risk, experienced in the past, in this approach is inflated results. US states compete to attract companies, but the federal government cannot offer the incentives China's central government can. The net effect is far more intense competition across provinces in China than in states across America.

★ ★ ★

ECONOMIC RELATIONSHIP BETWEEN THE US AND CHINA

★ ★ ★

Before exploring the relationship between the US and China on trade, investment and talent, we should begin with China's economic exposure to the world and vice versa. If we aggregate trade, technology and capital exposures, China's exposure to the world shrank by 25% between 2000 and 2017. Meanwhile, the world's exposure to China increased by a factor of three.[19] This reflects the boom in China's domestic economy, which drove the world to beat a path to China's door and China to reduce its exposure to the US sharply. This reduced exposure is evident in each of the three dimensions of trade, investment and talent, and will likely continue in light of the US declaration in 2017 that China was the greatest strategic threat to the US.

TRADE

The US attention on its trade deficit, importantly excluding services, where the US retains substantial trade surplus, has never been higher than during the current trade war. Ironically, this increased attention is coming as China's trade surplus dropped from 10% of GDP in 2007 to 1.3% in 2017.[20] As a consequence of the trade war, China has looked to reduce its trade with the US and increase trade with countries like Japan, Israel and Italy, as well as developing countries.

While the US is raising tariffs on Chinese goods and pushing China to increase its imports from the US in agriculture, energy and other sectors, it may be a case of winning the battle but losing the war. China's average tariff rate of 3.8% is 50% higher than the global average of 2.6%.[21] While the economics of tariffs are relatively inconsequential to the Chinese economy, the second order effects of lower consumer confidence and unemployment could be problematic.

The US restrictions on China's access to high technology is predictably leading China to accelerate its efforts to become less dependent on the US. The other impact of the trade war will be consumer prices in the US, as it's well recorded that consumers, not producers, bear the majority of costs when tariffs increase. This forces consumer prices up and drives demand down for those goods. The touted goal by the Trump administration is the return of US manufacturing jobs, which is dismissed by major corporation leaders who indicate they will find lower-cost alternatives abroad rather than shift those jobs back to the pricey US. How the trade war plays out remains an open question. The key issue for the US is access to the huge Chinese market, which is of far greater consequence than tariffs. Whether the US can win greater access through the trade negotiations or wind up losing current access is to be determined.

INVESTMENTS

Every country wishing to invest in the US must now go through the Committee on Foreign Investment in the United States (CFIUS), which monitors the degree to which foreign countries are investing in US businesses and developments that could pose a threat to the US. Apart from these CFIUS restrictions on Chinese deals with US companies, the US also looks to contain China in technology on two other dimensions. The first is to persuade its allies to apply constraints like CFIUS to any deal China may seek in the tech space. The second is similar in nature, which is trying to keep Huawei out of deals with US allies in the emerging 5G space in mobile communication. Huawei is the global leader in 5G technologies, the next-generation telecommunications network. 5G will be an intensely competitive technology globally. The US claims China's government could use Huawei's network to breach data security systems of Huawei customers and is trying to persuade other countries to not purchase Huawei equipment for the that reason. How much influence the US exerts over other countries is unclear given its current, aggressive 'America First' position. Whether this security concern is real or a cover for impeding the growth of Huawei is unclear.

Additionally, while not generally understood, less than one percent of the US's foreign direct investment (FDI) goes to China.

The largest sources of FDI to China are Korea, Japan and Taiwan. Likewise, FDI from China to the US in 2018 dropped by 90% from 2017 and continues to fall in 2019.[22]

TALENT

Beyond technology deals, a closely related issue is talent. The US is tightening visa requirements on multiple dimensions, including for highly educated scientists. Currently, approximately 60% of Chinese students return to China after their US education.[23] Beyond that, many Chinese scientists are working in corporations or university labs in the US. If US restrictions on scientists and science majors continue, China is likely to accelerate its efforts to convince and incentivize them to return to China. Separately, we can expect foreign universities to set up high-tech labs in China. Given the progress China continues to make in this space, clamping down on talent transfers is unlikely to deter China's focus on advanced technologies and many scientists suggest it would hurt US efforts.

★ ★ ★

BOTH ECONOMIC MODELS ARE HISTORICALLY HIGHLY SUCCESSFUL AND RESILIENT

★ ★ ★

On paper, the two economic models could not be more different: bottom-up, free enterprise capitalism in the US and top-down, government-directed control in China. But, if we examine a level deeper, we see similarities in the models. While the US set out to be minimalist with respect to business, the level of government involvement from trust-busting of monopolies in the early 20th century to the proliferation of regulations, imposing tariffs and tightening of controls over M&A, few corporations would describe the US government as uninvolved. And, while the Chinese government oversees all dimensions of the economy, the engine of growth continues to be the private sector, where the government's direct involvement to date has been modest at best. China's influence over SOEs is extensive, but SOEs have ceased to be the economic engine. So, should we be surprised that these two different but converging models have both been successful?

The historic contexts for performance are very different. The US economy has been the largest globally for roughly 150 years, which marks its industrial revolution in the late 19th century. Apart from the scale of its economy, the US also provided global leadership in a wide range of technology-driven industries, including aerospace and commercial airlines, biotech, telecommunications, information technology, social media and the internet. The US also leads most of the major service sectors globally from law, IT service, healthcare, advertising to accounting and consulting. Not surprisingly, the US leads the league tables of the most valuable global companies, with 126 out of the top 500 global companies as of 2018.[24] Finally, the US is the driving force behind the globalization of trade through the WTO, as well as the globalization of finance through the World Bank, IMF and the big US banks. The US uses the dominance of its banks globally to exert pressure on countries to support US sanctions on countries like Iran.

China's record is also impressive, but over a far shorter time frame: the last 40 years, when its industrial revolution began under Deng. China increased its GDP an average of 10% per year, significantly greater than that of any other major country during that time period.[25] Obviously, China's high growth reflects its low starting point, but its current growth rate in excess of 6%, off the second largest GDP base, is well ahead of that of any major Western country. China is also catching up to the US in terms of the top 500 global companies. That China is neck and neck with the US today in most of the advanced technology industries, with the exception of semiconductor manufacturing and biotech, suggests that the US and China will be the dominant economies for many years to come.

In addition to high levels of performance, the US and Chinese economies have proven to be quite resilient. The economic model of bottom-up, capitalistic free enterprise remained relatively unchanged through a series of major events including: the Great Depression of 1929; anti-trust action to break up monopolies in oil, steel, telecoms, railroads, etc.; World War II; the assassination of John F Kennedy; the Vietnam War and civil riots; the dot-com bubble in 2001; the September 11 terror attacks and the wars that followed in the Middle East and the Global Financial Crisis of 2008.

During these periods of crisis and change, the financial markets experienced periods of high volatility, where a number of major institutions failed and unemployment levels increased. Despite this, the economy rarely experienced negative growth due to steady increases in productivity and new, technology-driven markets. The underlying economic engine is strong and resilient. While the Chinese point to the 2008 crisis as an indication that the US economy is vulnerable, its strong recovery over the next 10 years reinforces its historic resilience.

China also experienced significant changes in its economy since the Chinese Communist Party took over in 1949: the Korean War in 1950; the Great Leap Forward in the late 50s, which led to famine that took over 30 million lives; the Cultural Revolution from 1966-1976, which shut down universities and took millions of lives, especially among the most educated; the Tiananmen Square riots in 1989; the Asian Financial Crisis; the Global Financial Crisis in 2008; and the war on corruption launched by Xi in 2012.

While the economy suffered many serious shocks before Deng launched the Reform and Opening Up period in 1978, the state-managed economic model endured. Many dramatic reforms took place that, while highly disruptive, enabled China to fundamentally restructure its economy and set the stage for several decades of, on average, double-digit growth in GDP.

While both economies are highly successful, they both face a number of uncertainties that could threaten future growth.

1. ADVANCED TECHNOLOGIES – WHO WILL WIN?

Given China's recent shift in focus from manufacturing for export of low-cost, mass-produced goods to higher-value-added products and services, the core strategic question is whether China is able to, over the coming decades, catch up to or pass the US in industries such as software, AI, semiconductors, advanced materials and biotech. The answers to the following questions will shape the outcome:

- Will the US's Darwinian model of thousands of startups, tens of billions spent by corporations on R&D, and strong, technology-focused universities continue to produce global leaders in new technologies as it has in the past?
- Will the US government need to invest in and coordinate private enterprise to some extent, as China is doing?
- How important will the following natural advantages be for China in this race?
  › Strong education system with increasing emphasis on mathematics and sciences. Will US visa restrictions undermine this advantage or accelerate it?

> › China is the largest consumer market globally and produced a growing number of global consumer giants over the past decade – Alibaba, Tencent, Baidu and Huawei to name a few. China also restricts access by foreign companies to their market. Will the West drive China to open up as part of a broader trade deal?
> › Rapid growth in research and development spending – China increased R&D spending by over 12% in 2017 alone, steadily closing the gap between themselves and the US for the most spent annually.[26]

- The Chinese government is investing heavily to support new technologies – will private enterprise in the US have the resources to compete, given the pressure from US investors for steadily increasing earnings? Will the major US firms cooperate in development or continue their head-to-head competition?
- The Chinese do not treat consumer privacy as a priority, unlike the US and Europe. How important an advantage will ready access to enormous volumes of consumer data be for the Chinese as they develop AI capabilities?
- Many Chinese scientists studied and remain abroad. Will China be able to attract top scientific talents back to China through some combination of incentives and nationalism?
- The US has a five- to ten-year advantage in chip manufacturing, which is a critical capability for many advanced technologies. Will China's huge announced plan to invest $140 billion in AI enable it to catch up in chip manufacturing?

While who will 'win' is emotionally important to some, most pundits believe the two countries will remain the global leaders, with one leading in some fields and trailing in others.

2. RAPIDLY AGING POPULATIONS: TO WHAT EXTENT WILL THE HUGE INVESTMENTS REQUIRED TO PROVIDE A COMPREHENSIVE SOCIAL SAFETY NET DEPRESS FUTURE ECONOMIC GROWTH RATES?

Almost 16% of the US population is over 65 today. That percentage is likely to increase to 22% by 2050.[27] Close to half of Americans have not saved enough to maintain their standard of living during retirement. Social Security and Medicare programs are reasonably mature, but both are underfunded and require significant financial support and/or a politically challenging increase in the retirement age. How big a drag on the US economy will those costs be?

Ten % of China's population is currently over 65 and that percentage is projected to grow to almost 28% by 2050.[28] China's social safety net is underdeveloped as is its healthcare delivery system. China is investing in both but has a long way to go. Counterbalancing a weak safety net is the high consumer savings rate – over 35% – in China and the tradition of children caring for parents. This strong cultural emphasis on family ties and responsibility plays a key role in understanding the Chinese people's savings rate. While the strain on China's economy will be real, the resilience of Chinese people has overcome many severe challenges, insinuating that China will adapt.

Key unanswered questions are:

- Will the Americans who are able to choose to work longer or accept a lower standard of living? Or, would the sizable senior voting population apply political pressure to improve benefits at the expense of economic growth?
- Will the large population of aging Chinese have saved enough to be relatively self-sufficient and/or

be supported by their children? How will the one-child policy's impact on family structure affect the outcome? This is referred to as the '4-2-1' challenge: four grandparents, two parents, supported by one child.

- Will the Chinese government, corporations and investors build low-cost retirement villages to relieve housing costs for the elderly?

3. FREE TRADE MODEL: WILL THE FREE TRADE MODEL, LARGELY IN PLACE SINCE THE WTO, GIVE WAY TO A PROTECTIONIST TRADE ENVIRONMENT?

Obviously, this is a huge issue in the global economy, but particularly for the US and China, who are the two largest partners in trade. If economic rationality ultimately prevails and free trade is re-established, the outcome should be a win-win for both countries. But, if the US feels threatened by the China 2025 Initiative on the question of leadership in high-value-added technology industries historically dominated by the US, a trade war could endure.

How vulnerable will China be to US trading actions? China's trade with the US has declined steadily as a percent of its total trading activity. This trend is accelerated as the BRI gains traction. At some point the US leverage could become inconsequential.

Will China open its markets to the US as part of a trade deal? This issue is of far greater economic import than the short-term economics of the trade war. Major US corporations understand this; whether the politicians do is another question.

4. HIGH DEBT LEVELS: TO WHAT EXTENT WILL THE HIGH AND GROWING DEBT LEVELS IN THE US AND CHINA CONSTRAIN ECONOMIC GROWTH?

The US debt took a jump recently to 105.4% of GDP, driven by the $1.5 trillion tax reform package recently passed by Congress. While historically high, it is well less than half that level in China as a percent of GDP, with unofficial estimates putting debt at around 300% of GDP. China claims that deleveraging the government and businesses is a priority, but deleveraging always dampens growth rates. The question is whether either country will see growth slow as a result over the next few years. China's advantage in deleveraging is that its economic growth is over double the rate in the US, so it's in a better position to absorb the impact than the US is. China also has far more flexibility in dealing with debt because it is all internal and subject to government control. Much of the US debt and currency is held by countries and institutions outside of the US, resulting in far less flexibility than China has.

5. XI STAKED OUT A NUMBER OF POSITIONS VERY DIFFERENT FROM DENG'S – WILL THEY DEPRESS OR ENCOURAGE ECONOMIC GROWTH?

Given Deng's economic track record, taking contrary positions seems risky. On the other hand, China is in a far stronger position today than it was when Deng began. The key differences are:

- Deng's philosophy included a low profile. Xi is creating a cult of personality not unlike Mao.
- Deng expected the Party to stay in the background and not get involved in operations. Xi declares the Party as pre-eminent.
- Deng installed term limits, believing two five-year terms was the right answer. Xi changed the rules, eliminating term limits.
- Deng supported the growth of private companies while shrinking SOEs. Xi champions SOEs and only came out supporting private companies after pushback against his pro-SOE position. A key issue will be the banks' willingness to lend to private companies. Some SOEs began lending to private companies at a spread above their costs.

The impact of Xi's policies may or may not impact the economy. A key question is what the impact of these policies will be on the confidence of investors in private companies. Time will tell.

6. TRUMP HAS ALSO TAKEN A NUMBER OF POSITIONS CONTRARY TO HISTORIC GROWTH DRIVERS. WILL THESE POSITIONS, GENERALLY OPPOSED BY CORPORATE AMERICA, HURT THE US ECONOMY OVER TIME?

The first is the trade war, which runs counter to the long-standing US commitment to free trade. Apart from correcting trade provisions that favoured the Chinese, the stated objective is recapturing manufacturing jobs. As noted earlier, this is unlikely to happen.

The second is the clampdown on immigration. This could hurt the economy on two dimensions. The first is a drop in unskilled labour that historically took jobs Americans were unwilling to take, like household help and farmwork. The second is highly educated immigrants who fill many key scientific and managerial roles in the US. Whether these policies stay in place and whether Trump gets re-elected are unanswered questions.

★ ★ ★

TAKING A
STEP BACK

★ ★ ★

Both China and the US have overcome a number of challenges to sustain strong economic performance, over the past 150 years for the US and the past 40 years for China. The challenges are daunting, but the track record suggests that betting against either China or the US is inadvisable. Further, the question of who will win is a very Western question based on the idea of a zero-sum game. The reality is that a booming economy in the US does not hurt China any more than a strong Chinese economy hurts the US. The likelihood is that China and the US will best each other in different economic sectors. The major change we can expect is the US increasing its commitment to protecting its own interests, which it failed to do during China's rise. China historically protected its own interests and will continue to do so.

CHAPTER
4

EDUCATION SYSTEMS: INCREASINGLY IMPORTANT, GIVEN THE GROWING ROLE OF ADVANCED TECHNOLOGIES

"No other investment yields as great a return as the investment in education. An educated workforce is the foundation of every community and the future of every economy."

– Brad Henry, former Governor of Oklahoma

As the US and China ratchet up competition in the high-value-added industries expected to drive economic performance over the coming decades, increased attention is focused on how well the education systems prepare individuals for those industries. Education systems are a major differentiating factor in a country's economic performance. The core differences between the two countries is that US primary schools are managed and funded at the state and local level and are under constant funding pressure, resulting in frequent cutbacks. China's schools are also managed at the local level, with central oversight, but treated as important strategic assets with the goal of constant upgrading. In this section, we explore the different historical and cultural contexts shaping the US and Chinese systems, highlight the differences and examine what can be learned from them.

EDUCATION - HISTORICAL AND CULTURAL CONTEXT IN THE US

Since the first US public school opened in 1635, the federal government's role in ensuring that school systems develop the talent required by for the US economy to be competitive has diminished. This is in line with the 'minimalist' governance model, which largely delegates education to state and local governments. There are two exceptions. The first is legislation passed in 1958 allocating $1 billion to upgrade math and science education following Russia's launch of the Sputnik satellite. The second is a report sponsored by Ronald Reagan, calling out the 'severe underperformance' of US schools.

The vast majority of federal action on public schools is related to social issues of discrimination by income, race, gender and sexual orientation. Attempts to introduce standard curriculum and make greater use of standardized testing have been unsuccessful. The actions taken at the state level are largely economically driven, leading to cutbacks and, recently, numerous teacher strikes. A major force in the education system is the United Federation of Teachers, established as a union in 1857. Its role in teacher qualifications, training, tenure and working conditions has been significant. Whether it succeeds in simultaneously protecting teachers and promoting better education is hotly debated.

Outside of public schooling in the US there is a large system of private pre-kindergarten through 12th grade schools as well, covering elementary, middle, and high school. This system of private schools accounts for 25% of all US schools and 10% of student enrollment and is diverse in terms of performance and stated educational goals.[1]

EDUCATION - HISTORICAL AND CULTURAL CONTEXT IN CHINA

As covered earlier, education was pre-eminent in the Confucian society. Individuals' responsibility was self-improvement through education to better support the family and society. Parents' primary responsibility was educating children and children in return owed parents obedience, respect and care in their old age. This 2,500-year-old focus on education was reinforced by the Imperial Examination System, which gave male students from all backgrounds, including the rural poor, the chance to attend top universities based on exam results. These examination and education systems focused on rote memorization, skewed to the Confucian classics, rather than critical thinking. Filial obligations led parents to be actively involved in children's education and instilled in students a strong commitment to not disappoint their parents.

Despite the turmoil in 19th and 20th century China, including the Cultural Revolution shutting down higher education from 1966-1976, the core design of the education system did not change materially until Deng's Reform and Opening Up. Deng realized that China had fallen dramatically behind the West, Japan, Korea and the Four Tigers because it failed to advance in manufacturing and technology. Schools accelerated attention on mathematics and the sciences, and later balanced rote memorization with critical thinking. Apart from shifting the education model,

Deng urged top students to attend university in the West, especially the top universities in the US and the UK. Finally, the One Child Policy increased pressure on parents and the commitment of the only child to perform.

Post-Deng, the Article 6 2001 Reform encouraged student participation by instructing teachers to ask questions and shifting classroom formation from rows of desks to a more interactive 'U' shape. Integrative thinking was incorporated. A second round of reforms for high schools came in 2018. The biggest change was an increase in elective courses from 26 out of 144 to 88 out of 144, so students could better pursue their interests. Teacher training shifted from memorizing facts to the 'how' and the 'why'. Case methodology, also imported from the West, emphasized critical and integrative thinking. Experiential learning, or 'learning by doing', was also introduced.

As China's role as the world's manufacturing exporter declines, in part because of lower-cost alternatives in Southeast Asia and robotics replacing labour, China's 2025 Initiative calls for investing in ten high-value-added advanced technologies, including AI, biotech, electric cars, high-speed computing, and advanced software.[2] The US sees the 2025 Initiative as a direct challenge, since the US dominates many of the ten targeted technology markets today.

In conjunction with the 2025 Initiative, ten advanced technology and scientific fields are prioritized and the brightest young students in these fields are selected for top universities. The proportion of secondary school students in vocational studies increased from 19% to 45% from 1980 to 2001, in response to an oversupply of college graduates and a shortage of highly skilled vocational workers.[3]

MAJOR DIFFERENCES BETWEEN THE US AND CHINA'S EDUCATIONAL MODELS

Six core differences stand out:

1. US EMPHASIS ON CRITICAL THINKING AND PERSONAL DEVELOPMENT VS. CHINA'S FOCUS ON ROTE LEARNING

The US classroom has historically encouraged high participation through questions, discussions and debates. The teacher's role is one of convening rather than lecturing. Collaboration and communication skills are fostered through class discussion and frequent group/partner projects. China's model before the 2001 reforms was teachers lecturing and students listening and memorizing, active participation wasn't encouraged. The transition to more interactive classrooms and critical thinking is under way, but given the scale of the system and the fundamental nature of the change, more time is necessary.

2. THE CURRICULUM IN THE US INVOLVES A WIDE RANGE OF ELECTIVES. CHINA HAS BEEN MORE STANDARDIZED, WITH EMPHASIS ON HISTORY, CULTURE, ENGLISH AND MATHEMATICS

The curriculum in the US is not nationally standardized; instead, it varies depending on state and local laws. Historically required courses on history and civics are no longer universally required. While China is increasing the number of electives it offers, Chinese history, culture, mathematics and English remain core.

3. WHILE THE US EMPLOYS STANDARD TESTS AS PART OF THE COLLEGE ADMISSION PROCESS, THE CHINESE SYSTEM RELIES ON TESTING ALMOST EXCLUSIVELY

The Student Aptitude Test (SAT) and the American College Test (ACT) are routinely and interchangeably used in the US in the college admission process, but they are one of many factors schools consider. The Gaokao exam in China determines what universities a student is eligible to attend, regardless of your GPA in school. While the Gaokao is the make-or-break exam in China, Chinese students are regularly tested and typically outperform their US counterparts when attending top-rated US high schools.

4. RESPECT FOR TEACHERS AND TEACHER QUALITY IS SIGNIFICANTLY HIGHER IN CHINA'S PUBLIC SCHOOLS

The 2018 Global Teachers Status Index ranks China number one out of the 35 developed countries for respecting teaching as a profession, while the US is ranked number 16. One component of this is a comparison with other professions; in China, teachers rank on par with doctors, holding the highest level of public respect.[4] Further, a British study found that Chinese teachers were on average recruited from the top third of college graduates, while US teachers are recruited from the bottom third.

5. CHINESE PARENTS ARE FAR MORE INVOLVED IN THE EDUCATION PROCESS THAN THEIR US COUNTERPARTS

Gauging level of support is difficult, but a number of inputs reinforce this conclusion. The first is the primacy of education in Confucian values. The second is the vast majority of Chinese families have only one child, primarily as a result of the One Child Policy. The third is a study showing that Chinese parents spend on average 15% of their income on tutors, weekend classes and other educational 'extras' vs. 2% in the US.[5] When in Beijing, I saw on the front page of the *China Daily* a photo of hundreds of parents cheering busloads of students off to take the Gaokao examination – a sight you would not see in America. I also learned of many students whose parents moved to a different hukou just to access a better school for their children.

6. THE UNIVERSITY SYSTEM IN THE US IS STRONGER, DEEPER AND MORE MATURE THAN CHINA'S

The university system in the US dates back to the 17th century and many universities have endowments of over $1 billion. The US has 33 of the top 100 universities globally vs. only seven in China.[6] China's universities are also largely state supported, while most of the top US universities are privately supported. Violence throughout the country delayed the development of China's university system during the first half of the 20th century and was completely halted during the Cultural Revolution from 1966-1976, contributing to its currently lagging position.

★ ★ ★

CHAPTER
5

★ ★ ★

HUMAN RIGHTS AND THE RULE OF LAW: US ABSOLUTIST IDEOLOGY VS. CHINA'S RELATIVIST APPROACH

"If you care about injustice,
and if you care about freedom,
and you care about human
rights, then you care about
them everywhere."

– Lara Logan, South African television and
radio journalist and war correspondent

My readings and discussions suggest that no issue between the US and China generates more heat and angst than human rights. The key to closing this gap is understanding three contextual differences underpinning each country's distinct path and present situation.

The first is the difference between an individualistic country and a collectivistic one. In an individualistic country, like the US, human rights are, first and foremost, individual rights. This goes back to the founding of the US, where individual rights were laid out in the Constitution and the Bill of Rights. In China, a collectivistic country going back thousands of years, the wellbeing of society and family take priority over individual rights. This mindset is grounded in Confucian values, which shaped China for over 2,500 years. This difference is fundamental and leads to very different outcomes on specific issues. As an example, the One Child Policy in China, which was viewed in the US as a gross misuse of governmental power, was designed to address the societal problems of overpopulation and resource shortage. The burden this placed on individuals made sense in China, because society as a whole would benefit from the policy. In the US, this encroachment on individual rights is seen as unjustified, regardless of the fact that, in China, many viewed this policy as a necessary evil.

A second contextual difference is the US absolutist approach to human rights vs. China's relativist approach. The US approach is a natural response to the lack of human rights the colonists and the Founding Fathers experienced in Europe. As a reaction, human rights are considered absolute and inalienable and were spelled out by the Founding Fathers in 1789. China's approach to human rights was heavily influenced by the suffering of its people in the 20th century. Over 100 million people lost their lives to foreign invasions, the Taiping Rebellion, chaos during the warlord period, the Civil War between the Communists and the Nationalists, the famine in the late 1950s that took over 30 million lives, and the upheaval of the Cultural Revolution. In response, the Chinese focused first on the basic needs of food, clothing and shelter, prioritizing the development of human rights behind these basic needs. Human rights as we know them today didn't begin to seriously develop in China until Deng took over after the Cultural Revolution in 1978. Since then, China made great progress in expanding human rights for its citizens.

A third factor is the age of each country and its current government. In the US, the government structure only ever existed as it does now. There have been no military takeovers, no coups and no radical change in the structure of the electoral democracy we know today. This doesn't mean it can't happen, as the US is a very young country, but many Americans express frustration and anger towards the system that has endured thus far. China, on the other hand, is a very old country with a deep history. It has experienced change in government when the current government didn't meet the needs of the people and provide stability numerous times throughout its history. Therefore, the Chinese Communist Party, which rules today and has existed for roughly 100 years, places a strong emphasis on social stability. The turmoil of the 20th century, ending with the Tiananmen Square demonstrations and violence in 1989, led the government to prioritize preventing disruptive actions, including protests, inflammatory speeches and the assembly of large groups. These preventative actions have been prioritized over human rights. To the Chinese government, the societal stability and prosperity over the past 30 years make the encroachment on individual rights worthwhile. In the West, these preventative measures are seen as serious overreactions and suggest a level of paranoia that is difficult to understand.

Beyond these contextual differences, human rights continue to evolve in the same direction in both the US and China on a number of dimensions explored in this chapter: political rights, personal freedoms, the rule of law, religious rights, minority rights, LGBTQ rights and women's rights.

* * *

THE FUNDAMENTAL, SHAPING ROLE OF INDIVIDUALISM IN THE US VS. COLLECTIVISM IN CHINA IN THE DEVELOPMENT OF HUMAN RIGHTS

* * *

In the US, individualism is all about 'the little guy'. The American dream is centred on rags-to-riches stories of individuals who overcame adversity to achieve success through their own talents and persistence. These heroes achieved greatness in all walks of life, including inventors, entrepreneurs, artists, athletes, scientists, entertainers and many others. The more adversity they overcome, the more they are celebrated. While heroes and heroines are celebrated for what they accomplish, the support of family and friends is typically overshadowed.

This mindset is also present in American stories of individuals treated unfairly by the judicial system. When the press highlights individuals triumphing over large corporations, doctors, hospitals or other major institutions, Americans will flock to support the individual. Individual rights and equal opportunities for all, while unevenly addressed in practice, are spelled out in the Constitution and Bill of Rights and enforced, in theory, by the rule of law. This protection was given to all citizens by the Founding Fathers in reaction to the lack of rights in Europe.

In China, the focus is first and foremost on the wellbeing of the family and society. While the difference between individualism and collectivism may seem to be one of semantics, the implication, when applied to specific issues, can be profound.

GUNS

In the US, the right to bear arms is protected under the Second Amendment. The proliferation of guns, including military assault rifles, results in the US having one of the highest levels of privately owned guns and close to the highest number of gun-related fatalities globally, close to 40,000 annually as of 2017.[1] This is one of the most contested individual rights in the US, with the majority of the population consistently polling for more restrictions on gun ownership. In China, the societal risk of private gun ownership outweighs the individual right to bear arms, which is true for almost every first world country.

DISSIDENTS

In the US, everyone has the right to express their political views, including views some would consider subversive. This mindset is consistent with a multi-party system incorporating a wide range of views that are protected by the individual rights of freedom of speech and freedom of the press. In China's one-party system, suggestions to improve the government's effectiveness or to set priorities are regularly solicited. Initiatives such as Charter No. 8, advocated by well-known dissident Liu Xiaobo, seeking to shift from one-party rule to an electoral democracy, are viewed as subversive and resulted in a life sentence for him. While his imprisonment resulted in protests globally, it did not in China. This reaction reflects the reality that the central government is broadly supported, in large part because it has delivered both prosperity and stability to China.

★ ★ ★

THE IDEOLOGICAL, ABSOLUTIST POSITIONING OF HUMAN RIGHTS IN THE US VS. THE PRAGMATIC, RELATIVISTIC POSITIONING OF HUMAN RIGHTS IN CHINA

★ ★ ★

A core difference between the US and China, with important implications for human rights, is how each country approaches an issue. The US focus on ideology is driven by Judeo-Christian dualistic values: right and wrong, heaven and hell, winners and losers. China's oriental values focus on harmony and balance rather than extremes.

In the US, human rights are described as absolute and inalienable. While the position of the federal government and its rulings on issues is inalienable, rights enforcement is typically left to the states. This leads to highly uneven application of voting and other rights based on sex, race, sexual orientation and even age. An example would be women's rights, which lagged behind male rights by more than a century in many cases and to this day are not universally enforced.

One factor contributing to the absolutist approach to human rights in the US is the stable conditions in the country. Secure borders throughout the major expansion period of the 19th century and abundant natural resources ensure that the basics of food, clothing and shelter have always been, by and large, broadly available.

China takes a different, less absolute approach when addressing human rights. Insecure borders, especially in the north, and the struggle of feeding the world's largest population with a limited amount of arable land meant basic needs were prioritized above human rights. The central government set its priorities in accordance with Maslow's hierarchy of needs. As a result, top priorities were food, clothing, clean water and shelter. This prioritization didn't ignore human rights, but it meant they were a lower priority than life's essentials. At a societal level, the government served the people of China well on a number of core dimensions:

- Over 850 million Chinese have been lifted out of extreme poverty[2]
- Life expectancy increased from 43 years to 76 years in just half a century[3]

- Adult literacy increased from 66% in 1982 to 96% in 2015[4]
- Infant mortality rates dropped from 8% in 1970 to less than 1% in 2017[5]

After addressing basic needs, the Chinese government held off on establishing clear human rights until it established the rule of law and the ability to enforce them. This approach is fundamentally different than in the US, where the voting laws, anti-discrimination laws and other human rights laws are established at a national level sometimes decades before effective enforcement is aligned at the local level.

★ ★ ★

LACK OF POLITICAL FREEDOM IN CHINA UNDER ITS ONE-PARTY SYSTEM IS THE CORE SOURCE OF MORAL CONFLICT WITH THE US

★ ★ ★

A core feature of the US political system is the ability to protest against the government, enabled by the freedom of speech, the freedom of the press and the right to assemble. The spirit of these freedoms is clearly articulated in Tocqueville's *Democracy in America*, as part of the 'minimalist' role of the government. This includes checks on government power guaranteed by the balance of power across the three branches, an adversarial multi-party system, elections every four years and the right to openly protest against the government.[6]

When the US challenges China on human rights, the heart of the challenge is centred on the issue of political freedom as defined in the US. What many do not understand is that the Chinese people have the right to object to government policies and practices. They do not, however, have the right to take actions viewed as undermining the government. If we examine the issue of political freedom from the perspective of the Chinese, the overthrowing of a government delivering prosperity, stability and increasing personal freedoms doesn't make a lot of sense. Instead, the Chinese people are regularly polled by the government, much like in the US, on their attitudes towards key policy issues and government priorities. A lack of tolerance for undermining behaviour, however, does not justify dissident mistreatment. The life sentence given to Liu Xiaobo, who advocated replacing the one-party rule with an electoral democracy, is not necessarily difficult to understand with respect to China's laws. But Liu's treatment was inhumane, especially denying him access to medical care before he succumbed to cancer.

While directionally, many Chinese people agree with the government's legitimate right to protect its one-party model, many would argue that the resources and means applied by the government go well beyond what is rationally justified by anything but a high level of paranoia. The government spends more on internal security than defense, which is puzzling when it has no credible external or internal threats. The censorship of the press and the internet is at an all-time high, despite the ease with which most skirt the internet censorship.

Have governments in China been toppled over the past four thousand years? Absolutely, but the common denominators have been broadly based on a loss of support of the people through ineffective leadership, corruption, inability to protect the country from external threats, inability to feed the country and insufficient response to natural disasters. While the ends, like ongoing prosperity and stability, may justify the means, the extreme focus on internal security in the absence of credible threats raises questions in people's minds as to the underlying motives.

★ ★ ★

BEYOND POLITICAL FREEDOMS, CHINA CONTINUES TO EXPAND PERSONAL FREEDOMS

★ ★ ★

The gap in personal freedoms between the US and China in 1978 (the year of Deng's Reform and Opening Up) was substantial, but it is narrowing. The Western press typically highlights censorship and restrictions on assembly, but the general consensus from Chinese people, when asked about limits on their personal freedoms, is that they can do what they want and not experience meaningful constraint in their everyday life.

The evolution of the 1958 hukou registration system is the prime example of personal freedom expansion in China over the past 40 years. The original hukou system, employed by centuries of rulers in China, monitored and managed population flow as well as administered taxation and conscription. The primary goal of population management was controlling the flow from rural to urban areas, which offered better housing, healthcare, education, employment opportunities and living standards. The hukou system, at certain points in time, determined who survived and who didn't. Of the estimated 30 million who perished from starvation in the 1956-1958 famine following the Great Leap Forward, 95% were in rural areas, with the limited food supply channeled to urban areas and those with an urban hukou.[7]

The 1958 hukou system tracked family births, marriages, deaths and had approval power over employment, housing and travel. Deng significantly relaxed the system by eliminating many of the differences between the rural and urban hukou, relaxing travel restrictions to smaller cities, opening up international travel for students and delegating more decision-making to local government. Currently, the hukou system limits housing, healthcare, education and employment opportunities for migrant workers in urban areas. The rationale for the ongoing constraints is largely economic; the government lacks the financial resources to open up urban services to all migrants working in major cities. Security concerns about having migrants becoming too large a proportion of urban population is another factor.

That being said, the government is currently increasing resources available to support migrant workers in urban areas.

Another important dimension of personal freedoms is the ability to travel. In recent years, the hukou limitations on travel within China have been largely eliminated and international travel increased dramatically. The original momentum for international travel was Deng's Reform and Opening Up initiative. He recognized, after the Cultural Revolution and Mao's death, that China's economy was left behind by many of the developed countries of the West, as well as Japan and the Four Tigers of Southeast Asia (Hong Kong, South Korea, Taiwan and Singapore). Encouraging international travel was one element of his initiative to get China participating in the global conversation, however, the heart of the issue was China's lack of technology. Deng actively cultivated China's relationships with the developed countries to get access to technology, but he also actively encouraged Chinese students to study in the West. What started as a trickle had grown from 144,000 in 2007 to 608,000 in 2017.[8] Over 60% of Chinese students in the US return to China after completing their studies abroad.[9]

THE RULE OF LAW IS STEADILY TAKING HOLD IN CHINA, BUT THE JUDICIAL SYSTEM IS ACCOUNTABLE TO THE CHINESE COMMUNIST PARTY, NOT INDEPENDENT FROM IT

When exploring the rule of law in the US and China, understanding the different contexts and mindsets is important. The US Constitution incorporated the rule of law from day one, reflecting its well-established position in Europe. The strong focus on ideology meant laws were enacted to represent the aspirations of those who drafted them. Frequently, however, not a great deal of attention was given to the system's ability to implement the law. Examples of this include the right to vote and equal pay. In China, the opposite is true, with the overwhelming focus on the pragmatics over the ideological. For this reason, civilian laws are generally not put into place until the Chinese authorities are capable of administering them. Even then, these laws are still subject to interpretation by the government if they become an issue of stability.

Prior to the collapse of the Qing dynasty in 1911, government officials settled major disputes at senior levels of the central government and minor disputes at the local government level. Individuals with the best connections, or 'guanxi' as it is known in China, and the greatest clout generally prevailed. Bribery also played an important role in determining outcomes. The rule of law was first established shortly after the end of the Qing dynasty, but the warlords period and the ensuing civil war meant these laws existed only as a formality for some time. Mao initially approved the rule of law, but quickly banned all lawyers after concluding that laws, and lawyers, were inherently hindering the control of the party.

Deng was the first leader to successfully implement the institutional rule of law between 1978 and 1981. One of the challenges was to recruit, educate and train high quality lawyers and judges. The first step was to reopen law schools at universities in 1979; next the All-China Lawyers Association was established in 1986 with the first official licensing exam; the first law firm was established two years later in Shanghai. The population of lawyers grew, but the vast majority of civil cases continued to be settled through less formal measures such as arbitration, collective action and mediation.[10] As of 2007, China only had about 118,000 licensed lawyers, equal to about one lawyer per every ten thousand citizens.[11]

While the number of practicing lawyers continues to grow in China, the gap between the US and China is huge. The US has roughly one lawyer per 300 citizens.[12] However, this is also reflective of the US attitude towards the law, which has historically been very open to adjustment and interpretation on a case-by-case nature. This also reflects the ability individuals, corporations and the government have to challenge each other and the law within the US. This kind of rule of law doesn't exist in China as we know it.

While China's population of trained lawyers and judges continues to grow, the pace of change within the law varies significantly. For example, laws related to international transactions receive far more attention than most areas of domestic law. In the international arena, China's legal capabilities are moving towards international norms on trade, supply chain management, and corporate and securities law, reflecting the impact of rapid globalization on trading, volumes, global supply chains and global corporate transactions. China's activity in the global economy is also facilitated by its increased level of participation in global institutions such as the WTO, the World Bank, the IMF and the Asian Development Bank.

While China is making significant progress on the international front, domestic progress is slower. The most obvious reason is that China needed to adopt international norms to protect its huge global trading business and its growing corporate transactions globally. China's natural interest in adopting Western norms domestically declined dramatically after the financial crisis of 2008, which China largely managed to avoid. Instead, China is moving ahead on domestic rule of law in a manner consistent with its history and priorities on the following issues:

CRIMINAL LAW

China's criminal law continues to modernize through its approach to sentencing, which applies software to analyzing sentences by type of offense. The goal is to improve the consistency and equity of sentences across jurisdictions. China's top-down model drives changes through this system across its vast network. The US recently passed its own prison reform bill, entitled the 'First Step Act', to reduce inequities in the system.

PRIVATE PROPERTY

Developing effective laws to protect private property has been a priority since individuals were first given the right to own land in China. A core challenge is addressing the abuses of developers, teaming up with local officials, to take land from farmers and other citizens without fair compensation. When the 'disturbance' classification system was discontinued, a high proportion of the 'local disturbances' involved land disputes between landowners, developers and local governments.[13]

FREEDOM OF SPEECH, THE PRESS AND THE INTERNET

This issue is, ironically, very black and white in China. The Chinese government has complete discretion in deciding whether individuals, corporations or organizations are taking action viewed as potentially undermining the government. Whether a particular article or speech or gathering criticizing the government (there are many) crosses the line into undermining is completely subjective. A number of subjects that reflect poorly on the government, like the Great Leap Forward, the Cultural Revolution, the Tiananmen Square riots and the jailing of Liu Xiaobo, cannot be written about or discussed in public forums. While government crackdowns receive a great deal of attention in the West, they typically do not in China. This is in part because the one-party system doesn't accommodate an alternative government and has, over time, delivered on its two core priorities: prosperity and stability.

While the West agitates over the treatment of dissidents and dissident lawyers, which is incredibly harsh by Western standards, the average Chinese citizen is largely disinterested. Unlike the effectiveness of the criminal justice system and private property rights, there is little motivation for the government to relax its historic principles on freedom of speech, the press and the internet.

CONTRACT LAW

Contract law exists in China but, apart from international issues where China is Westernizing rapidly, it is developing slowly. A vast majority of domestic disputes are settled informally or through arbitration rather than through court proceedings. This model is consistent with the historic norm of settlement by government officials based on an individual's standing, his or her relationships and, in some cases, bribes.

In the West, lawyers would question whether this informal approach can result in justice, which is a fair question. The Chinese, however, know that relying on a contract in court is a high-risk proposition, and so, as mentioned in Chapter 2, individuals rely far more on trust and relationships when entering into deals than on contracts. The model which produces the most just outcomes is far from clear. The fact that China has just under one lawyer per ten thousand citizens suggests that it lacks the legal resources to move in the Western direction even if it wanted to.

Apart from China's stance on each of these domestic issues, many in the West note the absence of an independent judiciary. The judiciary is overseen by the National People's Congress and is, officially, subject to China's constitution. In reality, the National People's Congress is seen by the West as a rubber stamp for the higher-level governance committees. Starting with the Central Committee, the Chinese Communist Party interprets the Chinese Constitution as it sees fit. If we look at this issue in the US, similar questions can be raised on the independence of the judiciary.

The appointment of the Supreme Court has become highly politicized, with Republicans looking to appoint conservatives and Democrats looking to appoint progressives or activists to interpret the Constitution. The voting records of the Supreme Court Justices, with respect to politically charged issues, suggests that, in practice, the independence of the judiciary can be called into question.

★ ★ ★

BOTH CHINA AND THE US STRUGGLE WITH THE TREATMENT OF MINORITIES

★ ★ ★

A core component of human rights is minority treatment, especially because a high proportion of human rights violations involve minorities. When exploring the treatment of minorities in the United States and China, explaining contextual differences is vital to understanding the underlying beliefs that shape these relationships. Three key differences are present here.

The first difference is how different groups became minorities. With the exception of African Americans, who were originally brought over as slaves, minorities immigrated to the United States by choice. The key minorities today originally migrated from South America, Africa and Asia. In the US, these minorities are dispersed throughout the country, creating pocket communities that retain their original culture, food, traditions and religions. These communities, and their dispersion, are the key behind the idea of the American 'melting pot'. In China, the minority populations occupied independent countries before they were annexed by China. The major minorities (Tibetans, Muslims in Xinjiang and Mongolians) never left their land or culture, but did have to adapt to a new governance model.

Secondly, the strength and role of the central government are fundamentally different. In the US, with its minimalist central government, the role with respect to minorities was to ensure, over time, equal rights and opportunities under the law. Enforcement, however, was delegated to state and local governments. Because of this, laws like voting rights for African Americans, instituted in 1869 under the 15th Amendment, were not implemented effectively for decades in some areas due to state and local resistance. Additionally, in terms of housing, education and employment, the US central government still struggles to close the standard of living gap for minorities. The degree to which minorities are dispersed throughout the US makes this particularly difficult. In China, the strong central government focus was on raising the standard of living (literacy, education, healthcare and housing) for minorities, just as was done for the majority Han population.

Because the central government retains superiority over all local governments, and due to the fact that minorities are largely isolated within specific regions, this initiative was far more effective in China, leading to increased minority quality of life.

Finally, the core identity in each country is very different. The US is a self-proclaimed melting pot and always has been. The country was built by immigrants coming from Europe, Africa as slaves, Asia in the 19th and 20th centuries and South America, largely in the 20th and 21st centuries. These immigrants settled throughout the country, with different densities in different states. The core value for immigrants entering legally was equal rights and opportunities under the law. In China, the population has always been dominated by the Han majority, who number over 93% today. Though the territories annexed by China are now governed as autonomous regions, they benefit from the same centrally driven efforts, enabling the core Han population to raise its standard of living. The Chinese government, though nominally protecting minority cultures and religions, is steadily increasing the Han influence in minority territories by resettling Han Chinese and appointing Han Chinese to senior government positions in these territories.

With these three core contextual differences in mind, the treatment of the minority population in each country can be judged on three bases. The first is the granting of basic rights and, through them, the objective of minimizing discrimination. The second, and more pragmatic lens is how effectively were those rights put into practice. The third is how significantly did the minority standards of living improve.

African Americans make up 12.6% of the US population as of 2017, making them the second largest minority group.[14] The US's horrific treatment of African slaves as property began when they were first brought over in 1619 to work on plantations in the eastern colonies. Their status as property was officially affirmed by the Dred Scott Case in 1857, which ruled that all blacks, slaves as well as free, were not and could never become citizens of the United States. Just four years later, in 1861, the Civil War began and culminated with the abolition of slavery in the US. Following the end of the Civil War, a number of constitutional amendments and acts of Congress granted rights to African Americans and spelled out actions to prevent discrimination on the basis of race. The 14th Amendment, ratified in 1868, granted citizenship to all African Americans born in the US. The 15th Amendment, ratified in 1870, guaranteed the right to vote and prohibited any state from denying the right to vote on the basis of race, colour or prior servitude.

Although this amendment is officially the law of the land, states in the South effectively prevented African Americans from voting for decades through a combination of polling taxes, ID requirements, literacy tests, property requirements or intimidation at polling places. This prompted the nationwide Civil Rights Movement, including marches, protests and demonstrations beginning in the 1940s and gaining momentum over the next two decades before culminating in the late 1950s and early 1960s with Martin Luther King Jr. In response, a second wave of federal legislation was initiated to protect the rights of African Americans with the Civil Rights Act of 1964, which prohibited segregation in public places and banned discrimination in employment. The following year, the Voting Right Act in 1965 prohibited state action impeding voting rights. The Fair Housing Act of 1968 guaranteed equal access to housing regardless of race or colour. The key challenge for the US federal government was enforcing these laws across the entirety of the United States, something it simply didn't, and doesn't, have the capability of doing without state and local support. This second wave of non-discrimination laws reduced, but did not eliminate, discrimination; it all depended on the level of local enforcement.

So, on the first dimension of granting citizenship and related rights to African Americans, no action was taken until after the

North prevailed in the Civil War, roughly 240 years after the first slaves arrived. Those actions were not effectively enforced in the South until the Civil Rights Movement and second round of federal legislation in the 1960s. In this case, the minimalist role of the central government, as depicted by de Tocqueville, and the counterbalance between states' rights and local prejudices led to a nearly 100-year period before enforcement was given high priority. To this day, efforts to reduce minority voting, such as gerrymandering, and housing and employment discrimination, continue.

If we step back from rights and their enforcement and observe the evolution of the standard of living for African Americans in the US, we see progress, but meaningful gaps persisting between blacks and whites. African American median income was $31,100 vs. $48,000 for non-Hispanic whites in 2016.[15] The African American college graduation rate is 38% vs. 62% for whites.[16] The unemployment rate is almost four points higher than the rate for white Americans.[17] Incarceration rates are five times higher for African Americans.[18] The underlying story here is relatively clear. While the US government has provided equal rights to African Americans, discrimination at the state and local level impedes progress in closing gaps on living standards.

Immigrants from South and Central America make up the largest minority racial group, at 17% of the total US population in 2017.[19] Latinos who attain citizenship in the US receive full rights of citizenship and legal protection from discrimination, as is the case with every other citizen. Per capita income for Latin Americans is similar to African Americans ($30,400 vs. $31,100) despite being in the US for far less time. This doesn't include the approximately 11 million Latinos who entered and reside within the US illegally, who obviously don't have those rights and are therefore vulnerable to housing and employment discrimination. The macro conclusion for these two major minority groups is, while great progress has been made in federally legislated rights, the impact on standard of living continues to lag by significant measures.

Asian Americans are the third largest minority population in the US, representing 5.2% in 2017.[21] Their history in the US includes several dark periods. The Chinese emigrated in the 19th century, looking to capitalize on the gold rush in the western United States and also providing the labour to build the trans-continental railroad. Many Americans believed the cheap labour from China was taking American jobs. As a result, the Chinese Exclusion Act was passed in 1882, prohibiting all immigration of Chinese workers to the US. This was reversed in 1923. The dark moment for the Japanese in the US was their internment in 1942 following the Japanese bombing of Pearl Harbor. A later investigation under President Jimmy Carter found internment to be racially motivated and unconstitutional. Those interned were later given compensation. Today, Asian Americans report higher income levels than the white population.[22] Contributing to this are higher education levels and, in some cases, a level of affluence before immigrating to the US.

Despite the lagging standards of living for many minorities living within the US, strong representation of different cultures and minorities across the country is what gives the country its reputation as a 'melting pot'. Chinatowns exist in nearly every large city in the US. Chicago dyes its river green each year on Saint Patrick's day. Just over 13% of the US speaks Spanish at home.[23] In Miami, over 75% of residents speak a language other than English at home, with Spanish being the most common.[24] There are countless examples of minority foods, clothing, customs, languages, religions and cultures across the US due to centuries of assimilation by immigrants from around the world. While this sprawl and dispersion makes it difficult for the federal government to ensure that minorities are guaranteed all the rights they are entitled to as citizens, cultural and ethnic diversity across the US has always existed and is something to be celebrated.

There is, however, an incredibly dark stain on the US treatment of minorities that should be recognized, which is the mistreatment, discrimination and persecution suffered by the Native
Americans. What began as the clash between Native American
culture and colonial culture cumulated with the US violently
forcing the Native Americans to leave their native lands for the
West and, ultimately, reservations. Beyond violence, this native
population also succumbed to diseases brought from Europe to
the Americas. Their persecution continues today with the building of pipelines through sacred grounds and flagrant disrespect
for the autonomy guaranteed to them by law. The decimation
of the Native Americans follows the textbook definition of gen-
ocide and led to numerous formal apologies on behalf of the US
government and the American people in 1993, 2000 and 2009
for a "legacy of racism and inhumanity".[25] These circumstances,
while fundamentally different from the evolution of today's significant African American, Latino American and Asian American
minorities, but must be recognized as a deeply shameful piece of
US history.

Turning to China's treatment of minorities, we can examine
the two largest minority regions – Tibet and Xinjiang.

Each of these countries became part of China in the 18th century and have remained part of China since, with the exception
of brief periods of independence during the Chinese Civil War in
the mid-1900s. As mentioned earlier, each of these autonomous
zones were and continue to be inhabited by people with their
own customs, language, culture and religion. That being said,
despite being declared autonomous, the Chinese central government retains control of the regions, encourages Han Chinese to
relocate there, and has placed Han Chinese officials in positions
of power within these regions. China's stated goal is to protect
minority histories and identities, subject to the overarching goal
of maintaining stability and improving education, healthcare,
housing and overall standard of living.

Against the goal of improving the standard of living, China continues to make significant progress. In terms of maintaining stability, it has been less successful. Both Tibet and Xinjiang are challenging regions for the Chinese government due to deeply held religious beliefs in those areas. Inner Mongolia, by contrast, remains relatively stable.

Tibet was absorbed into China in 1720, declared its independence in 1940, China re-established control by invasion in 1950 and Tibet was declared an autonomous region in 1954. Protests against Chinese occupation broke out in 1956, during which the Dalai Lama fled to India with 80,000 of his followers. China decisively suppressed the uprising, resulting in many deaths. Following this event, the government embarked on a major program of land reform, converting Tibet from its historic feudal model, under which nearly all land was controlled by monks served by commoners. Protests flared up again with the 2008 Olympics, during the carrying of the Olympic Torch around the world. Dozens of monks were beaten, incarcerated and killed as part of the protest.[26] The protest became violent in Tibet in the following days, resulting in more deaths as well as extensive destruction of property.[27] Since then, Tibet has been relatively stable, but over 150 monks have committed suicide by self-immolation in protest of Chinese control since 2009.[28]

Violence also flared in the autonomous region of Xinjiang, which is largely inhabited by Muslims with strict religious and dietary practices. While ethnic tensions triggered periodic protests, suppressions increased after the 9/11 terrorist attacks in the US, leading to more significant protests and reprisals. In 2009, a major protest took place in the capital city of Urumqi triggered by a brawl between native Uyghurs and Han Chinese living in the area. The clash resulted in 140 deaths, 828 wounded and hundreds of Uyghurs taken into custody.[29] In 2013, a car driven by Uyghurs plowed into tourists in Beijing, killing five and injuring dozens in the crowded area.[30] In Kunming, railroad station knife attacks carried out by Uyghurs left four dead and 130 wounded, leading to further crackdowns, including a life sentence for a prominent Uyghur scholar.[31] More recently, hundreds of thousands of Uyghurs in Xinjiang have been detained in internment camps, subjected to brainwashing techniques intended to undermine their Islamic beliefs as well as violence.[32]

Despite these incidents, China has managed to measurably improve the standard of living in the five regions with the highest populations of ethnic minorities. Some of the indicators include an improvement in literacy rates since 1950, when education became compulsory, reducing illiteracy an average of 50% across minority groups, but still lagging far behind the Han majority.[33] Total economic output in autonomous regions grew from roughly 3.66 billion RMB in 1949 to over 850 billion RMB in 1998 – an incredible improvement in just under 50 years.

Stepping back from the treatment of minorities in both the US and China, we see a mixed story. While the US has succeeded over time in legislating broad rights for minorities, the enforcement of those rights has been poor, in part reflecting the strong role of state and local governments in enforcement as a part of the minimalist government model. On the broader issue of standard of living, both African Americans and Latinos continue to trail whites on the basic measures of income per capita, education and literacy. Some would say the government is not doing enough to close those gaps. Many others would say the government's role is to ensure equal opportunities for all, but that state and local governments and communities must do their part to ensure these laws are practiced and respected.

The story is also uneven in China, but the underlying drivers of the treatment of minorities are quite different than in the US. Given China's strong, central government and focus on driving higher prosperity for all, China has lifted more than 850 million people out of extreme poverty.[34] It has also grown the economy an average of 10% per year over 40 years and continues to grow the economy at a rate more than double that achieved in the vast majority of developed countries.[35] The area of contention obviously comes from China's focus on stability and readiness to crack down quickly and forcefully on uprisings or terror-related incidents. Though the number of incidents and fatalities is incredibly low when compared to the larger population, the constraints on personal freedom that come from pervasive surveillance, the use of internment camps and imprisonment do diminish what China has accomplished in raising the quality of life among its minorities.

★ ★ ★

LGBT RIGHTS IN CHINA LAG FAR BEHIND THE US AS OF 2019

★ ★ ★

While not an ethnic minority, the LGBT communities in the US and in China faced their own battle for rights and recognition.

The history of LGBT rights in the US is a far more winding road than in China because of states rights. In the US, states' rights allowed for different treatment of the LGBT community throughout the country and over the decades. For example, Illinois decriminalized homosexuality in 1961, while it remained illegal in the state of Texas until a 2003 Supreme Court ruling deemed it unconstitutional. President Bill Clinton signed the Defense of Marriage Act in 1996, banning same-sex marriage federally. Just a few months later, a Hawaii judge ruled that the state did not have a legal right to deprive same-sex couples of the right to marry. The real win for LGBT rights came in 2016 when the Supreme Court legalized same-sex marriage nationally, and then in 2017 when the 7th Circuit Court of Appeals ruled that the Civil Rights Act prohibits discrimination based on sexual orientation.[36]

In China, the story of LGBT rights is much shorter and less publicized. In 1997, the National People's Congress decriminalized 'hooliganism', assumed to include homosexuality, and in 2001 China removed homosexuality from the list of recognized mental disorders.[37] However, the Chinese Communist Party never publicly made statements concerning its lack of rights, including the right to marry, and discrimination faced by the LGBT community in China. The community receives no special protection or recognition by the government, but does not face outright persecution. Without specific commentary, the sentiment by the government towards the LGBT community seems to be tentative tolerance but no special protection. However, open LGBT orientation remains socially taboo, and without government protection, individuals are likely to face discrimination socially and professionally.[38]

While the US has managed to provide more rights for this social minority, violence and discrimination are still prevalent across the country where state and local governments neglect to enforce federal law. In this respect, China lags behind the US as it has thus far failed to recognize its LGBT minority and ensure it is protected by law from discrimination and prejudice.

* * *

AFTER SUPPRESSION OF RELIGIOUS FREEDOM UNDER MAO, THESE FREEDOMS ARE GROWING

* * *

Freedom of religion in the US was a core objective of the Founding Fathers and a direct reaction to the religious persecution dominating Europe at the time. Religious freedom is explicitly guaranteed by the Constitution and the Bill of Rights. While religious minorities exist throughout the US, roughly 70% of Americans identify as Christians, creating a significant majority. Roughly 23% do not identify with a specific religion or are either atheist or agnostic.[39]

While the necessity of the separation of church and state is recognized, many legal skirmishes have taken place on references to God in pledges and the existence of prayers in school. Despite this specific issue, the core issue of freedom of religion in the US has been largely unchallenged. Violence in houses of worship occur intermittently, but frequently the motivator is either racial or religious bigotry, with the law and local community intervening aggressively in those instances. In short, freedom of religion remains a core tenet of being American and has never been seriously challenged. The story in China is somewhat different.

Historically, China has three dominant religions/philosophies: Confucianism, Taoism and Buddhism, which was imported from India.

In addition to these three pillars of religion and philosophy in China, Western missionaries exposed China to Western religions beginning in the 17th century. While the missionaries believed they were enlightening or saving the Chinese by teaching them Christianity, many in government felt they were trying to convert the Chinese, because the West regarded them as heathens, and undermined China's history and culture.

If we fast-forward to Mao and Communism, there's a strong anti-religious bias. In part because the party saw Communism as an all-encompassing way of life with no room for religion, but also because the communists were suspicious of any large, organized group with the potential to become a threat. Western missionaries were not welcome, but the deeply ingrained philosophies and beliefs of the three pillars lived on, though more under the radar. This peaceful coexistence changed during the Cultural Revolution, with Mao empowering the Red Guards to attack anything grounded in the past. Hundreds, if not thousands, of Taoist and Buddhist temples and monasteries were destroyed and Confucius' grave was disinterred.

More recently, the Chinese government is becoming comfortable with Eastern religious groups, going so far as to rebuild temples that, over time, have become tourist attractions. The exceptions are Western churches, which recently have been required to remove crosses from the tops of buildings. The other exception is Falun Gong, which is a spiritual practice founded in 1992 which combines meditation and breathing exercises with the tenets of truthfulness, compassion and forbearance. The number of practitioners grew to over 70 million by the late 1990s. In 1999, without government knowledge, it organized a major march on the government demanding change. The government responded with a strong suppression and, to this day, the Falun Gong are banned in China.[40]

The majority of Communist Party members are atheists, which sets the tone for religion in China. While the government doesn't explicitly support religions, it is increasingly tolerant. A 2010 Pew Research Center report suggests that close to 22% of the population practice Taoism or some form of folk religion, 18% identify as Buddhists, 5% are Christian and almost 2% are Muslim. Classifying by specific religion is complicated in China because of overlaps in belief and the fact that few consider their spiritual beliefs and practices 'religions', as many are more philosophical or spiritual in practice.[41] In effect, forms of religion and spiritual practices are broadly practiced in China with minimal government interference, with the exception of religious-based protests or uprisings.

Religious freedoms in the US have been a given, with a large majority of government officials having a religious affiliation.

In China, government officials are avowed atheists and religious freedoms were directly attacked during the Cultural Revolution, though today the government is very lenient. What both countries have in common is a largely religious/spiritual population practicing their beliefs and existing free from government interference.

★ ★ ★

WOMEN'S RIGHTS EVOLVED ALONG SIMILAR LINES IN THE US AND CHINA

★ ★ ★

Both countries significantly expanded women's rights over time, but the shift happened slowly. While the rights are broad and discrimination is outlawed, women are continually underrepresented in senior ranks of corporations and government in both countries. Some point to discrimination by men in positions of power, some attribute it to the natural consequences of women's perceived role at home and raising a family, and others hold the questionable belief that women lack the mindset or skills to take on senior leadership roles.

In the US, the first major milestone for women's rights occurred in 1900, when all states recognized a woman's right to own property. In 1920, following the Suffrage Movement, women were granted the right to vote. The Equal Pay Act was passed in 1963, promising equitable wages for the same work regardless of race, colour, religion, nationality and sex. In 1964, Title VII of the Civil Rights Act prohibited sex discrimination in employment, in 1965 married couples were granted the right to use contraception, and in the still contentious ruling of Roe vs. Wade in 1973 abortion was legalized in all states subject to state-by-state restrictions.[42]

As with the issues of equal rights and anti-discrimination against minorities, enacting laws is one thing, enforcing them is another. Issues like workplace discrimination, equal pay and maternity leave are prevalent across the US, with little being done to address them en masse. Two areas where this distinction is most stark is the advancement of women in business and government and the recourse of women subjected to sexual harassment and assault.

A few statistics reinforce that women have been restricted from advancing in their careers to the same levels as men in the US. In business, 25% of executives, 20% of board seats, 6% of CEOs and 22% of law partners are women. In government, 25% of state legislators, 10% of governors, 20% of mayors of major cities, 21% of senators and 19% of the House of Representatives are women. Several of these numbers have increased with the 2018 elections, which saw over 100 women elected to the House of Representatives.[43] The overall conclusion is that women are underrepresented, given that more women complete a college education than men in the US and occupy an equal proportion of entry level positions.[44]

The second major area of discrimination is sexual harassment and assault. Again, the issue is not a question of rights but of enforcement. Historically, the burden is on the woman to prove her case, but in cases of 'he said, she said' the man is far too often given the benefit of the doubt, escapes without jail time or penalty, and the victim's reputation is tarnished in court and later the community. These outcomes have led many women to not press charges. This phenomenon recently sparked the #MeToo movement, which gained momentum after the successful prosecution of a number of prominent executives in the entertainment, sports, education and corporate world, encouraging many women to speak out.

While the history and evolution of women's rights is quite different in China, the current position in the two countries is similar. Confucius defined the woman's role as subservient to the male. When women married, they lived with and became part of the groom's family with the wife serving under the direction of her mother-in-law. The vast majority of marriages were arranged between the families based on family needs and socio-economic status. Gifts and dowries were generally part of the marriage agreement, and when the husband died the wife belonged to the husband's family. Apart from being considered subservient to men, women were often subject to the horrific process of footbinding, beginning in the 13th century – in part because tiny, lotus-shaped feet were regarded as attractive and because men preferred women to be less mobile. The practice of footbinding was made illegal in the early 20th century.

The subservience of women to men was eliminated under the Chinese Communist Party. Under the Marriage Law, enacted in 1950, women were free to make their own choice of a spouse but, as with many enacted rights, execution was difficult to enforce. The right to a lawful divorce was granted in the Marriage Law of 1981 and the party subsequently approved equal pay for equal work.

In 2005, domestic violence was officially designated as a crime in China. As with sexual harassment, sexual assault and domestic violence in the US, how effectively this is reported and prosecuted is problematic and depends on the individual situation.

Though the Chinese Communist Party granted extensive rights to women in the 20th century, the impact of the one-child policy included numerous negative consequences for women. The most obvious was the number of abortions and the infanticide of girls by parents looking for a son to carry on the family name and, for those in rural areas, to do the heavy lifting on the farm. The policy was relaxed multiple times, with the ability to have a second child by paying a fine, the right of two married single children to have two children of their own, and finally relaxing to two children being allowed for a married couple by 2016. Despite this, the legacy of this policy and decades of cultural preference towards men over women has left a lasting impact today. Nearly 40 years later, out of China's population of 1.4 billion, there are nearly 34 million more men than women.[45]

Beyond equal rights for women, the Party invested in the education of women by making nine years of schooling compulsory. A major effort was launched to sharply reduce the rate of illiteracy among women, especially in rural areas. The results of these efforts have been compelling, with the 51% literacy rate for women in 1982 improving to over 94% by 2015.[46]

In terms of advancement of women to senior positions in business and government, China has done slightly better than the US with a penetration rate of 30% vs. 25% in the US. The one area where China does not perform well is at the most senior levels of government. No women are on the most senior body, the seven-person Standing Committee of the Politburo, only one woman is a member of the 25-person Politburo, and only 10 women are on the 205-person Central Committee.[47]

HUMAN RIGHTS IN THE US AND CHINA

While many see human rights as the defining difference between the US and China, looking at human rights by category, personal freedoms, political freedoms, rule of law, treatment of minorities and treatment of women, the differences are modest with the exception of political freedom, which is explained by China's one party system, which always opposes actions viewed as undermining the system.

For the vast majority of Chinese, personal freedoms are approaching those in the US. China is catching up in the rule of law, especially considering it was only instituted in the early 1980s under Deng. China's progress is dramatic, given the relatively short period of time, on international issues and is also significant, though less so, domestically. China can be criticized for the lack of an independent judiciary, but the US also struggles with the impact an increasingly polarized two-party system has on the independence of the judiciary and its rulings. China's hukou system continues to limit access to public services for migrants in cities, but this is an economic issue, not human rights.

Giving either country the edge in the treatment of minorities is difficult. The US treatment of Native Americans is textbook ethnic cleansing. While African Americans have equal rights today, continuing discrimination by local and state governments is pervasive and little has been done by the federal government to improve their standard of living. Additionally, no coherent immigration policy is established to address the treatment of millions of Latinos who have entered the US. China has materially improved the standard of living of minorities living in the five autonomous regions, but maintains an oppressive level of surveillance in Tibet and Xinjiang and has actively undermined the practice of the Muslim Islamic religions through discrimination and the use of internment camps. The US does, however, recognize and protect its LGBT minority, something the Chinese government has yet to do.

On the issue of women's rights, both countries have, over time, provided equal rights of voting, property ownership, marriage rights and employment, including equal pay for equal work. Though these rights are guaranteed by both governments, enforcement continues to be an issue. Both continue to struggle in the advancement of women into senior level positions and protecting women from sexual harassment, assault and domestic abuse.

The major difference in the end is political freedom, which is closely linked to freedom of assembly, speech, the press and the internet. Each of these freedoms is fully protected in the US. In China, these freedoms are granted at the discretion of the government, meaning actions considered to be inflammatory or undermining the government do not fall under this protection. While the Chinese government's actions against activities meeting the 'undermining' criteria are heavily criticized in the Western press, the reality is China's one-party system serves the Chinese people incredibly well and enjoys one of the highest government approval ratings in the world.

If the lack of political freedom were an important issue for the Chinese people, this concern would register in their support of the Chinese government. Pew Research Center Political Landscape surveys consistently show support levels that are among the highest of any major country, and far higher than those given by Americans for the US government. Presumably, the high ratings in China reflect first and foremost its economic performance, but the level of support would likely indicate if the Chinese people were genuinely angry about a lack of political freedoms. It appears more reasonable to assume high ratings are a reflection of a government serving its people well. Alternatively, the low scores for the US government can be taken to reflect the challenges the US minimalist government experiences in affecting change and enforcing the law within its adversarial two-party system.

In summary, examining human rights at a more granular level, and understanding the three important contextual differences cited at the beginning of this chapter, leads me to conclude the differences are less dramatic than most assume and many of those differences are understandable.

CHAPTER
6

FORMS OF DEMOCRACY: US ELECTORAL COMPARED TO CHINA'S RESPONSIVE TO THE PEOPLE

Democracy (n): government by the people; rule of the majority; a government in which the supreme power is vested in the people and exercised by them directly or indirectly through a system of representation, usually involving periodically held free elections.

– Merriam Webster

The Founding Fathers created the US as an electoral democracy with the approval of the Constitution in 1789. The ultimate goal was life, liberty and the pursuit of happiness for each individual American. This goal is supported by the ancient Judeo-Christian belief that each individual, as a son of God, has dignity and worth and is equal to every other man.

During one of my visits to China, I was surprised when a senior government official responded to my description of democracy in the US with the statement, "China is also a democracy, but we have a different definition. For us, democracy means, 'responsive to the people'." What he means here is, while China has no free elections except at the local level, the government invests great effort to understand and meet the needs of the people.

The goals are similar: the people's wellbeing. However, the focus of America's definition is each individual, reinforcing the individualistic culture of the US. The Chinese definition focuses on the 'people' collectively, reinforcing its collectivistic culture.

The means are also different. In an electoral democracy, the focus is on actively participating by voting to create a government by and for the people. The means in China are not through popular elections. Instead, the Chinese use polling and other tools to learn the needs and priorities of the people and use the feedback to shape government's decisions and actions.

In this chapter, we explore the historical context of democracy as defined by the US and by China, as well as how effectively each functions in relation to its goals.

EVOLUTION OF DEMOCRACY IN THE UNITED STATES

Prior to the War for Independence, Great Britain ruled the 13 Royal Colonies through Crown-appointed governors. Self-government existed at the town and county level, but Great Britain determined important economic matters, like taxes and duties. Voting in the colonies was limited to white male property owners. The colonies followed the traditional English model of three branches of government (executive, legislative, judicial), English rule of law, and the court system.

Following the victorious War for Independence, the Founding Fathers developed the Constitution to anchor democracy in the right to vote, giving the American people a power they never had in Europe. This early voting system granted few citizens the opportunity to participate directly in government other than at the local level. When designing the voting system, the US government sought a compromise between two extremes. The first is direct election by popular vote, ensuring everyone's vote counts with equal weight. The second is election by the legislature, similar to China's current model. In this system, senior officials, including the President, are elected by the most senior party officials.

The compromise solution was the electoral college system, whereby each state was given electoral votes equal to the number of senators and congressmen from the state, favouring less populated states. However, a critical design decision allowed each state to decide whether the electoral votes split in proportion to the direct vote in the state or the winner takes all.

The former is more aligned with the core principle of 'every vote counts' and has equal weight. The latter is not, given a winner with 51% of the votes takes 100% of the electoral votes. Not surprisingly, all states but Maine and Nebraska opted for the winner-takes-all model, maximizing the states' impact on the election's outcome.

The proportional voting system is theoretically more consistent with the spirit of democracy: in practice just two elections occurred where the winner of the popular vote lost the election: 2000, when George W. Bush beat Al Gore, and 2016, when Donald Trump defeated Hillary Clinton.

The winner-takes-all model gives roughly six to ten 'swing' states (states with high uncertainty of outcome but typically account for under 20% of the total votes) de facto control over the outcome. This leads candidates to focus most of their resources on the swing states and depresses voter turnout in the non-swing states.

A second feature of the system undermining the core value of a representative democracy is gerrymandering. Gerrymandering allows the party in control of the state to redraw district boundaries to their advantage. Therefore, the party in power may capture only 51% of the vote, but win 75% of the seats. Gerrymandering allows political clout and self-interest to undermine the popular vote of the people. To the winner go the spoils. A number of states outlaw gerrymandering, but many do not.

THE RIGHT TO VOTE STEADILY EXPANDED OVER TIME

Under the original Constitution, only white male property owners had the right to vote. Thomas Jefferson stressed the importance of ensuring that the electorate was knowledgeable, which led to the limiting criteria for the right to vote.

All states eventually removed the property owning requirement by 1856. In 1870, the 15th Amendment established that the right to vote could not be denied based on race, colour or prior servitude. In 1920, the right to vote was extended to women under the 19th Amendment and, in 1924, it extended to include Native Americans and Chinese immigrants.

The last major expansion was in 1971, when the age limit was reduced from 21 to 18 on the basis that, if you're old enough to serve in the armed forces, you are old enough to vote.[1] The last frontier is whether or not former felons are able to vote. This debate continues to this day.

MANY STATES HISTORICALLY ENACTED LAWS TO PREVENT MINORITIES, TYPICALLY AFRICAN AMERICANS, FROM VOTING. THE VOTING RIGHTS ACT WAS DESIGNED TO FIX THIS

Despite the 15th Amendment, a number of states, mostly Southern, enacted voting requirements intended to prevent African Americans from voting. This included voter IDs, literacy tests and polling taxes. Some went further and closed polling sites in African American neighbourhoods. Beyond formal restrictions, many citizens attacked or intimidated African Americans at polling places. The Voting Rights Act of 1965 made these practices illegal, but new initiatives with the same intent continued. Despite impediments, African American voting rates are close to those of the white voting population in recent elections, trailing by only four percentage points.

CONSTRAINTS ON CAMPAIGN FINANCING ARE INCREASINGLY WEAKENED

Until the Citizens United Case in 2012, campaign finance laws and rules starting in the 1880s put increasing restrictions on campaign contributions and their disclosure. In the Citizens United Case, the Supreme Court ruled campaign contributions by corporations and individuals were protected by the First Amendment. Unsurprisingly, this lead to a huge influx of money into campaigns. The amount of campaign money in congressional races increased over 600% from 1980 to 2012, and money for presidential campaigns increased over 1,200% in the same time frame.[2] Combined with how much 'free' media such as Trump realized through his appearances in the news – estimated at $2 billion – the amount of money in political campaigns has skyrocketed in recent years.[3]

The extensive role of media now enables presidential candidates with extensive marketing skills and personal appeal to defeat candidates with far greater political experience. Examples of this include Donald Trump and Barack Obama, who defeated Hillary Clinton and John McCain, respectively.

HOW THE DEMOCRATIC SYSTEM PERFORMS IN THE US

The system is designed to give citizens a direct say in selecting leaders in government through voting in free elections. The expectation is that government decisions should, over time, reflect the will of the people. The system's performance is mixed against these different objectives.

VOTER TURNOUT IS LOW, ESPECIALLY CONSIDERING THE IMPORTANCE ATTACHED TO THE RIGHT TO VOTE

Given that the primary vehicle for participating in the governance is voting in elections, US voter turnout is surprisingly low, at 56% in the most recent presidential election and 50% in midterm elections.[4]

Among major democracies, the US ranks 26th out of 32 countries in voter turnout.[5] While precise data on why people choose not to vote is not available, experts offer a number of possibilities. The first is the effort and cost of voting outweighs the perceived benefits. Costs include taking time off work, waiting in lines and taking the steps required to register in each state.

Voter apathy also undermines the expected value of participating. Some voters are fed up with politics and don't engage in the political issues of the day. Some are unmotivated to vote because the key races are not competitive, given the number of states that consistently vote either Democratic or Republican;[6] the turnout in states with competitive elections is higher than in uncompetitive states.

Ethnicity and age also influence turnout rates. White and African American voters had 65% and 60% turnout rates in 2016, respectively, compared with 47% for Hispanic voters in 2016. Turnout rates are also significantly below average for younger voters. Seniors, aged 65 and older, had an almost 71% turnout rate compared with a 46% voting rate for those aged 18 to 29 in 2016.[7] Some countries attempt to solve this problem by making voting compulsory, with penalties enforced for not voting. Given the low turnout in the US and the emphasis on personal freedoms, moving to a mandatory model is unlikely.

GROWING PARTISANSHIP

On the objective of meeting the will of the people, the historic approach is for Congress to be a deliberative body, with the two parties finding compromises to resolve differences. Those days are gone, as partisanship dominates Washington and the legislative process.

According to David Boren, author of *A Letter to America* and former Oklahoma senator, a recent survey found that 83% of Americans find the nation so polarized between Democrats and Republicans that Washington can't make progress in solving major problems. Boren attributes the growing partisanship largely to recent changes in campaign financing. These changes allow two key things to happen. The first is the funneling of a growing proportion of the funds raised for single issues clearly dividing the parties, such as gun control and universal healthcare. The second is extremely wealthy individuals exerting undue influence by funding expensive media campaigns promoting candidates and issues they support.[8]

Most campaign funds go to senators and representatives who take the strongest positions on polarizing issues. They are also rewarded by the party with the most attractive committee assignments. The extremists reaping the rewards hollows out the moderates, with many in the middle opting out through retirement rather than continuing the seemingly futile role of forging workable compromises.

This partisanship led the Democrats under Obama to ram the Affordable Care Act (ACA), known as Obamacare, through Congress with little input or involvement from the Republicans. The Republicans under Trump returned the favour by trying, and coming one vote short, of repealing the ACA. The Republicans then crafted and passed tax reform legislation billed as a middle class tax break. If unchanged, the reform is estimated to funnel 83% of the accumulated financial benefits to the wealthy by 2027.[9] This legislation was developed without input from the Democrats and was passed, like ACA, along close to unanimous party lines.

The partisanship leads young people to lose interest in running for office. A well-known Washington journalist recently asked approximately a hundred students how many were interested in running for office. Almost no hands went up. When David Boren posed the same question to students, he heard, "It's all about the money. Those with the money win elections." And the money doesn't come from everyday people, it comes from political action committees (super PACs) and lobbyists. The role of money is reinforced by Boren's estimate that members of Congress spend a third of their time raising money instead of doing what they were elected to do.

THE WILL OF THE PEOPLE IS NOT BEING HEARD IN WASHINGTON ON A RANGE OF ISSUES

Opinion polls demonstrate a number of issues where the will of the people is ignored by Congress and/or the executive branch.

THIRD-PARTY OPTION

In response to today's partisanship, 62% of Americans recently polled felt it would be good to have choices in the next presidential election other than Republicans and Democrats.[10] As it stands, the electoral college absolute majority system would make a third-party presidential candidate an unlikely victor. The above discussed campaign finance reform further disadvantages a third party because the two established parties have a deeper base to finance their runs. A strong third -party base also seems impossible while the party can almost certainly not get a presidential candidate elected, but can act as a spoiler by pulling votes from the lead candidate, as Ross Perot did in 1992, enabling Bill Clinton to defeat H.W. Bush. While a successful third party is legally possible, neither Republicans nor Democrats show any interest in modifying the campaign and election ground rules to make a third-party option practical.

GUN CONTROL

Polls consistently show that the majority of Americans want stricter gun controls. This does not mean repealing the Second Amendment, but requiring strict background checks and banning assault rifles. Over the years, the National Rifle Association (NRA) consistently thwarts action on this issue, resisting any form of gun control and imposing its interests, aka those of its major donors, by giving ratings from A to F to congressmen and women based on their level of support for gun controls. It also makes millions of dollars worth of contributions to candidates who oppose all forms of gun control, spending $54 million in the 2016 presidential election alone.[11]

INCOME INEQUALITY

Income inequality in the US is at an all-time high, with 1% of the population controlling over 40% of wealth.[12] The drivers are extraordinary investment returns in the advanced technology sector (social media, search, software, e-trading, biotech, etc.), a steady reduction of marginal income tax rates, and few constraints on inherited wealth. That the most recent tax reform will funnel 83% of the economic gain to the wealthy, but 76% of Americans support higher taxes on the wealthy, indicates that the gap between the will of the people and congressional action is huge on this issue.[13]

SIZE OF THE FEDERAL DEFICIT

A new Rasmussen Report finds that 77% of likely voters think politicians' unwillingness to reduce government spending is more to blame for the size of the deficit than taxpayers' unwillingness to pay more taxes.[14] The most recent tax legislation added $1.5 trillion to the deficit and was roundly criticized by economists as unnecessary given the strong economy and that few of the benefits went to the middle class, who are more inclined to spend and therefore stimulate the economy. Tax breaks for the wealthy, immense military spending (the US accounted for 36% of global military spending in 2016, almost three times more than China)[15] interest on debt and social programs all contribute to the deficit. As the deficit is allowed to continuously grow, this issue remains at the forefront of voters' minds.

JUSTICE AND PRISON REFORM

By a two-to-one ratio, voters believe that the US relies too heavily on incarceration.[16] Fifty-five percent believe that the justice system discriminates against impoverished communities.[17] This is unsurprising considering that the US accounts for 5% of the global population and has 21% of all inmates worldwide.[18] According to the Marshall Project, voters also reject the 'War on Drugs' on principle and a solid majority support the federal legalization of marijuana.[19] A survey conducted by the Legal Action Center suggests that 63% believe too many non-violent drug offenders are incarcerated in lieu of treating addiction, and 78% said, "We need to treat drug and alcohol addiction as more of a health problem and less as a criminal problem."[20] Close to a decade later, the federal government recently passed justice and prison reform legislation with the 'First Step Act' at the end of 2018.

DESPITE ALL THIS ...

America's 230 years of democracy, though messy and irregular, has proven remarkably effective and resilient. Effective in the sense that the two overarching goals, a country shaped by a robust, free enterprise economy and strong human rights, are a reality. The US economy has been the strongest globally for 150 years and human rights continue to expand over the years related to race, gender and sexual orientation.

Most would argue that those core successes, coupled with the US's contributions in the World Wars and the establishment of key international organizations to deal with global issues, far outweigh the 'messiness' of the US democracy. The US democracy also has proved to be very resilient over a long period of time, surviving a brutal Civil War, major foreign wars, multiple presidential assassinations, the Great Depression, several financial collapses and global terrorism. The US model remains at the forefront of technology and healthcare breakthroughs and contributed to the betterment of the rest of the world for over 150 years.

EVOLUTION OF DEMOCRACY IN CHINA

China describes itself as a consultative democracy, and the Chinese People's Political Consultative Congress (CPPCC) was established in 1954 to implement this core idea. Little progress occurred under Mao's leadership period, given the turmoil of the Great Leap Forward in the late 1950s and the Cultural Revolution from 1966-1976. How Mao outlined the essence of a consultative democracy in his definition of the Mass Line Model is as follows:

"Take the ideas of the masses (scattered and unsystematic ideas) and concentrate them (through study turn them into concentrated and systematic ideas), then go to the masses, embrace them as their own, hold fast to them and translate them into action, and test the correctness of these ideas from the masses and once again go to the masses so that the ideas are preserved in and carried through. And so on, over and over again, in an endless spiral, with the ideas becoming more correct, more vital and richer each time."

Mao's thought is eerily similar to the core mantra of quality programs and continuous improvement schemes popularized by modern corporate management gurus in the past 20 years. The difference is Mao was applying this concept to the management of the country rather than the manufacturing of a product or the delivery of a service. While ideologically powerful, Mao did little to implement these core ideas into the management of the country by the Chinese Community Party.

CONSULTATIVE DEMOCRACY PUT INTO PRACTICE UNDER DENG
Unlike the US's 230 years of history with electoral democracy, the idea of a consultative democracy is only 40 years old, so today's model is largely still the model Deng enacted. Following Mao's Mass Line Model, Deng brought the idea to life by systematically collecting input from the people on a wide range of issues, large and small, and creating a test and learn environment where core ideas became workable before they were implemented.

With this approach, the people's voice in government, the core idea of democracy, is achieved through participation in formulating initiatives and in refining them in the real world to ensure that core objectives are met.

Obviously, this form of participation is very different from the US model of participation of selecting government officials through voting. The underlying differences are twofold. The first is that the focus in China is on the issue and initiative, whether it is building a road, establishing curricula for schools, or developing a model for delivering healthcare to the elderly.

In an electoral democracy, the ultimate decision is selecting an individual for a position, and with the individual comes a set of values and beliefs that, theoretically, shape decisions they make. The major difference with the US is that voting is an individual right, where every person chooses to participate in the governance process – whether they exercise that right is their choice.

In a consultative democracy, in a collectivistic society, not everyone has an opportunity to provide input on every issue, so the focus on getting enough input from the people affected by the issue to ensure a high level of confidence that the input accurately reflects the will of the people.

The two interpretations of democracy, ruling from the people, are very different. However, they have the same overall objectives: serving the wellbeing of the people and enabling people to shape, directly or indirectly, the outcomes through some form of meaningful participation. Where they differ the most is in their implementation.

The mechanisms China uses to collect the input from the people vary. While the media plays a greater and greater role in US political campaigns and races, the state retains control over the media system in China, reducing its volatility and potential impact on political outcomes. Rather than news polling and social media blasts from politicians, the CCP relies on more formal data gathering. The first, and most formal, mode of collection is through the CPPCC, which is made up of roughly 2,200 members. This includes representatives from the eight non-communist parties and individuals from various occupations, religious groups, the military and other significant segments of society.

The CPPCC gathers input on thousands of proposals by asking the members to canvas their natural constituents on issues of importance. The CPPCC then recommends, with input from the party, which proposals go through the National People's Congress for a decision. Many in the West say the CPPCC has little power because it doesn't make any final decisions. This perspective is grounded in the dualistic values of the West: decision-makers have power, advisors do not. The Eastern values of balance and harmony are much more amenable to an influence model, which is how the CPPCC operates. Beyond the CPPCC, a number of other important sources of input are tapped.

1. The Chinese Academy of Social Sciences, as part of the State Council, has thousands of researchers who regularly gauge public opinion on a wide range of issues. According to dozens of expert interviews I did in China, the Academy is highly respected and influential.
2. The ministries and regulators I interviewed indicated they spent significant time in public hearings and interacting with the public on proposals to change laws or regulations.
3. On geographic levels, provincial governments, major cities and, at the most local level, towns and villages hold regular meetings to discuss proposed changes, from micro-issues such as traffic controls to mega-issues like building a major dam.
4. There are 89 million members of the CCP, with many tapping into their networks and providing feedback to the CCP on recurring issues and priorities.[21]

While these sources may appear less concrete than the American system of polling, this does not make them less legitimate. Decisions at the government level in China happen behind closed doors, so pointing to any specific action and saying, "This came from this specific source of input," is impossible. However, the progress China makes as a country and the high level of public support implies that these issues and priorities are making their way back to the central government.

The government's five-year planning process provides a significant periodic opportunity to take stock of what has and hasn't worked and identify new forces changing priorities. Today these would include healthcare, pollution, education, Taiwan, proposed infrastructure projects, urbanization and others. Essentially, these domestic issues are given priority in both the US and China because they are close to home.

The discipline of this process, the involvement of experts from industry, academia and the government, and the debates and synthesis of conclusions all play a major role in shaping critical decisions on priorities, resource allocation and fiscal policies. From start to finish, the five-year plans take over 18 months to finalize. Additionally, progress against plans and sources of variances are regularly analyzed.

The election process under China's consultative democracy varies from the US model, but has some surprising similarities. While the US voting democracy literally has registered citizens lining up to vote for the highest office of president every four years, the majority of decision-making is in the hands of the elected representatives in Congress. The premise holds that elected officials represent the sentiments of their constituents and speak for them in Washington, DC. This includes voting on budgets, laws, policies, etc. Under the Chinese consultative democracy, 35 electoral units, mostly provincial-level People's Congresses, vote on the nominees for the position. This could be compared to the confirmation of a candidate for Supreme Court Justice in the US, where the President nominates someone he believes to be qualified and elected officials vote for or against the candidate, thus representing their constituents. Unlike the US, the NPC has quotas for representation in the National People's Congress by minority groups such as women, ethnic groups, military members, etc.

ON THE ROLE OF TEST AND LEARN

Deng was the champion of the test and learn model. China approaches most issues incrementally and the larger the stakes, the greater the testing before major decisions are made. One particular issue I consulted on in China was healthcare, which is a huge issue given China's rapidly aging population and the growing focus on health due to an increasing standard of living. The issues are highly complex, with government-managed hospitals, a shortage of facilities, Western health institutions interested in bringing the latest health technologies and drugs to China, and a lack of clarity on the role insurance companies play going forward.

China's response to this complexity is hundreds of experiments, pilots and start-ups targeting specific chronic diseases, and huge untapped opportunities concerning the use of AI to identify cost-effective treatments. This bottom-up, test and learn model is compatible with different solutions for different geographies and different customer segments.

The test and learn model also informed reform policies throughout the 1970s and 1980s as the Chinese economy shifted from a command-control system to introduce more free market influence and globalization. Rather than suddenly open their developing economy to international trade and competition, the government gradually opened Special Economic Zones (SEZs) where free market prices and power could operate. This allowed them to see how Chinese businesses and employees functioned outside of the command economy for the first time since the establishment of the PRC. Slowly, free market infrastructure expanded as the SEZs proved successful and popular, and the economy slowly transitioned based on how the 'test' cities performed.

While executing this model takes much more time than implementing big changes top-down, the risks are also much lower. Big, top-down solutions in the US, like Obamacare and immigration practices, typically generate many costly and unintended consequences which may have been avoided in a test and learn environment.

★ ★ ★

HOW CHINA'S CONSULTATIVE DEMOCRATIC MODEL PERFORMED

★ ★ ★

How input from the people gets translated into proposals and how critical resource allocation decisions are made is not transparent in China's corporate governance model. This is wholly unlike the US, where behind the scenes is, in fact, on stage for the world to see. In the absence of transparency, we can try to judge indirectly by examining economic performance, how economic performance translates to living standards for various socio-economic segments, expansions in personal freedoms, and the level of people's support for the government. On each of these indirect measures, China's consultative democracy model performs well.

★ ★ ★

STEPPING BACK
AND TAKING STOCK

★ ★ ★

Based on history, concluding that either of these two democratic models is not well positioned going forward is difficult to support. Many predicted upheaval or collapse in China and have been proven wrong. While democracy in the US faces a growing list of challenges, it continues to prove resilient.

So, what can we conclude at this point in history?

THE US DEMOCRACY IS INHERENTLY MESSIER THAN CHINA'S MODEL

A divisive two-party system with full transparency, a balance of power across the three branches, and presidential elections every four years guarantees a high level of ongoing disruption. China's leadership team, by comparison, is more cohesive and experienced, with no decision-making transparency. Further, China's test and learn model facilitates less risk taking and enables quick adaptation. Tensions arise from differences, but they remain behind closed doors and once decisions are made they are fully supported. Finally, the discipline of the five-year planning process ensures a balance between short-term operating issues and long-term investments. The US model makes producing a one-year budget difficult and leads to persistent underinvestment in the strategic areas of education, healthcare and infrastructure.

THE US GOVERNMENT IS RARELY POPULAR WITH THE PEOPLE

The Founding Fathers designed the US governance model to make government decision-making difficult so the free enterprise economy could thrive. Citizens, seeing dysfunctional behaviour by government officials through full transparency, are understandably unimpressed. This is reflected in the results of the Edelman Trust Barometer, an annual online survey that calibrates trust in governments, businesses, NGOs and the media throughout 27 markets and tapping into 1,150 individuals per market. To the question "Which institution is the most broken?" 59% of US citizens believe the government is the most broken institution. To the question "Which institution is most likely to lead to a better future?" 15% of US citizens, the lowest percent, said they believe government is the answer.[22]

THE CHINESE CENTRAL GOVERNMENT SUSTAINS A HIGH LEVEL OF SUPPORT FROM THE PEOPLE

The central government is in charge of all important decisions and actions taking place. The government delivered prosperity, stability and national pride over the 40 years of Reform and Opening Up, and it reflects the same in the Edelman Trust Barometer. To the question "Which institution is the most broken?" 38% of Chinese citizens believe business is the most broken institution. To the question "Which institution is most likely to lead to a better future?" 68% of Chinese citizens believe the government drives the country forward.[23]

THE US GOVERNMENT FACES MORE SERIOUS CHALLENGES TODAY THAN CHINA'S

The path to reverse the growing US partisanship is unclear. The resulting gridlock led to a sharp growth in the number and importance of executive orders, which shifts the balance of power from the legislative to the executive and judicial branches. Partisanship also undermines people's confidence in government and discourages talent from running for office. A second challenge, grounded in a Supreme Court ruling, increases the influence of exceptionally wealthy donors, frequently with extremist views, on election outcomes. Finally, the infighting, as well as ongoing deficit spending, is undermining the US's ability to make the long-term investments needed for future growth.

While China faces many serious issues, including an aging population, income inequality fast exceeding the US in scale, environmental pollution and technology gaps in chip manufacturing and elsewhere, a single-party government with strong leadership and an efficient corporate governance model is well positioned to deal with its challenges.

Despite this, the US and China's success in building the two strongest economies globally is tied to their own unique forms of democracy. Both will be challenged to a greater extent going forward as their rivalry intensifies and the technology-driven pace of change accelerates. How well each adapts will determine future successes.

The major challenge to understanding the two different forms of democracy is the lack of openness in the West to understanding China's model and recognizing how the current US model seriously compromises the original objectives of the Founding Fathers. In the bigger picture, the US is designated as the global standard bearer for democracy and China is recognized as the world's largest communist country. Beyond this broad perspective, there are many compromises to Jefferson's vision of one man and one vote for fully informed male citizens. If we look beyond the 'communist' label and recognize that the goal is to serve its people well, the 'responsive' Chinese model focuses on delivering prosperity and should be considered a credible alternative to a traditional electoral democracy.

CHAPTER
7

WORLDVIEW AND THE MILITARY: US FOCUS ON SPREADING DEMOCRACY AND HUMAN RIGHTS; THE CHINESE FOCUS ON ECONOMIC INTERESTS, NOT SPREADING A MODEL

"We grow up to respect the gray. Black or white, one or the other, is childish. It represents the worldview of someone who does not know the world."

– Richard Cohen (American syndicated columnist for *The Washington Post*)

The worldview and military involvement of the US and China could not be more different. The worldview of the US, first demonstrated by the Monroe Doctrine of 1823, is the promotion and safeguarding of democracy and human rights globally. This expansive worldview kept the US active on foreign soil for most of the past 125 years and almost full time over the past 50.

China hasn't shown any serious interest in hegemony over the past 2,000 years and consistently stays within its borders, with the exception of economically motivated activities. While China was defeated and humiliated by the West and Japan in the Opium Wars and the Sino-Japanese War, its engagements were focused on defending itself. China's aggression towards foreign countries over the past 1,000 years has been largely inconsequential: one invasion of Korea in the 17th century[1] and two in Vietnam, with no lasting impact.[2]

The impact of both countries' military involvement in foreign wars is significant in human sacrifice, shaping the world order following the World Wars, militarily for the US and economically for both. The US involvement in the Cold War and the War on Terror has cost over $10 trillion in current dollars.[3] China's involvement in the Opium Wars, Sino-Japanese War and the two World Wars delayed its participation in the global industrial revolution until 1980, roughly 110 years after the US.

In this chapter, we explore in greater depth the core of the two worldviews, the ensuing military involvement and where we go from here.

★ ★ ★

DEVELOPMENT OF THE US WORLDVIEW AND MILITARY INVOLVEMENT

★ ★ ★

While the Monroe Doctrine staked out a bold role for the US in the Western Hemisphere, the general military strength, particularly the naval strength, required was not sufficient to enforce it. The first time the Monroe Doctrine was brought to bear was in the Anglo-Venezuelan border dispute in 1895. The first time the doctrine was enforced by the military was in 1898 with the Spanish-American War, which led to the liberation of Cuba from Spain.

As part of the settlement with Spain, the US annexed the Philippines, Guam and Puerto Rico through a combination of a $20 million payment and the use of military force. During the same time period, but unrelated to the Spanish-American War, the US annexed Hawaii by force. The popular phrase used to capture the spirit of the US expansion into the Pacific is 'manifest destiny', championed by President Teddy Roosevelt. While never formalized as a doctrine or policy, the phrase embodied expansionism, exceptionalism and nationalism, and marked the US as a global power. This theme was fully embraced by the Democrats, who sought an ever-expanding role for the US, but was opposed by the other leading party, the Whigs, who believed the US should lead by example, rather than aggressive expansion.

The US's pivotal role in supporting the Allies in World War I and II established it as the strongest military on the planet. Post-World War II, a new era began, marked by the Cold War between the West and Communism, but more specifically between the US and the Soviet Union. The military conflicts driven by the Cold War include the Korean War (1950-1953), ending with a stalemate between North and South Korea, and the Vietnam War, ending in 1975 with the withdrawal of the US and its allies and the communist takeover by the North Vietnamese army. The Cold War subsided significantly with the breakup of the Soviet Union in 1991.

The most recent chapter in the US military's involvement on foreign soil involves the Middle East, beginning with the Iraq War in 1991. Triggered by Iraq's invasion of Kuwait and refusal to retreat despite a UN ultimatum, the war culminated in an aggressive US-led invasion ending with a ceasefire after roughly a month of hostilities. The War on Terror began in 2001 after the 9/11 attack on the US by Islamic extremists. In retaliation, the US attacked Afghanistan in 2002 and hasn't left since. The US subsequently engaged in a second war with Iraq after the takeover of that country by ISIS. Involvement with Iraq continues to this day and has spread to Syria, where the US has attempted to defeat ISIS to the point where its revival is impossible.

While popular support for the US involvement in World War I and especially World War II, following the Japanese bombing of Pearl Harbor and German aggression, was high, the support for involvement in Korea, Vietnam and the Middle East was mixed. Opposition to these wars has been on multiple grounds. Some believe the US attacking countries that have not attacked us is immoral. For others, fighting 'unwinnable' wars, like Vietnam, Iraq and Afghanistan, is foolish. For many, the enormous human and economic cost of war cannot be justified. The cold reality of wars since World War II is that the cost is astronomical, in excess of $10 trillion in today's dollars.

Whether for cost or moral reasons, the growing consensus in the US is we cannot police the world. President Trump is pushing an 'America First' agenda designed to sharply reduce US global military involvement. A core, stated objective is redirecting resources to tackling domestic issues such as crumbling infrastructure, healthcare, housing, education and paying down the debt.[4]

It's too early to tell if the 'America First' mantra means a fundamental change in the US worldview. Starting with the Monroe Doctrine, the US worldview has been essentially interventionist and expansive, engaging with countries whose actions harm the spread of democracy and human rights. The goal of this worldview was, with the exception of Pacific takeovers, the protection of America's interest and the spread of democracy and human rights. The goal is not to expand America's borders.[5]

★ ★ ★

DEVELOPMENT OF CHINA'S WORLDVIEW AND MILITARY INVOLVEMENT

★ ★ ★

China established its current borders in the 18th century through the takeover of Tibet, Xinjiang and Inner Mongolia. Taiwan was returned to China at the end of World War II. The shaping of China's borders parallels what happened in the US in the 19th century; the Louisiana Purchase, the acquisition of Florida from Spain, the treaty ending the Mexican-American War in 1852, and the purchase of Alaska. The expanding borders in both countries involved a combination of military aggression, friendly takeovers and outright purchases.

There are some governance issues within China's declared territory. One notable example is Taiwan, which is a part of China through 'one country, two systems' and the One China Policy, even though some Taiwanese continue to seek independence. However, the focus of this chapter is examining each country's worldview and military actions outside of each country's current borders and ongoing disputes.

China's declared worldview dates back over 1,000 years. Some believe it goes back 2,000 years to the Qin dynasty, which first unified China between 221 and 207 BC. The Chinese worldview today asserts that China's core objective is raising the standard of living for Chinese people, achieving stability, and that China isn't interested in acquiring foreign lands or interfering in the governance of foreign countries. China's track record is historically consistent with this worldview, with few small-scale exceptions, namely minor actions in Korea and Vietnam.[6] An interesting question in retrospect is what drove China to this insular worldview. A number of important contributors come to mind.

CONFUCIAN AND EASTERN VALUES

Eastern values, and Confucian values in particular, place a premium on 'wen' (harmony and respect) as opposed to 'wu' (violence and conflict). The social pecking order reinforces this, with scholars ranked first, followed by farmers, craftsmen, merchants and then the military.

CHINA AS THE CENTRE OF THE UNIVERSE

China called itself the 'Middle Kingdom' next to heaven, during its great dynasties. China remained the most advanced civilization in the world for most of its history. This superiority complex was reinforced by the tributary system,[7] which required leaders of other countries to visit the emperor, pay respects and offer gifts. This China-centric view was furthered by the Ming emperor, who decided to dismantle China's navy, the largest and most advanced in the world, in the 15th century.[8] Essentially, the emperor signified that China had nothing to gain by interacting with the rest of the world. When the English brought modern inventions and machinery to the Qing Emperor during the Opium Wars of the 19th century,[9] the response was effectively 'we have no interest'. This China centricity also reflects the mono-racial makeup of China, with the Han Chinese accounting for 93% of the population.[10] Foreigners were deemed 'barbarians' whose presence would compromise the racial superiority of the Han.

STARTING IN THE 19TH CENTURY, CHINA WAS CONSUMED BY FOREIGN INVASIONS AND SUBJUGATION

Over a span of 110 years, beginning in 1840, China endured the West's Opium Wars, the Taiping Rebellion, which claimed 10 million lives, the overthrow of the last dynasty (Qing), the rule of warlords, WWII, the Civil War ending in 1949, the Great Leap Forward, when over 30 million people starved to death, and the Cultural Revolution. Those internal and external conflicts, in addition to China's delayed industrial revolution and the challenge of feeding a huge, growing population, made foreign aggression impractical.

THE CHINESE WERE SKEPTICAL OF USING SCARCE RESOURCES FOR FOREIGN WARS

The Chinese government demonstrates a high level of pragmatism in its strategic initiatives over the last 40 years. This includes incentivizing businesses to increase productivity, modernizing farming through larger farms and technology, creating an export-driven manufacturing powerhouse, and building leadership positions in high value added high-tech industries.[11] These transformational changes were executed with China's modest resources. Deploying significant resources to foreign aggression made little sense.

★ ★ ★

WHERE DO WE GO FROM HERE?

★ ★ ★

While the historic worldviews of the US and China are polar opposites, they appear to be converging ever so slightly. As the US under Trump pursues an 'America First' agenda by pulling back from global organizations and treaties and withdrawing troops from long-running wars in the Middle East and Afghanistan, it moves closer to China's self-interest agenda. Whether Trump's first two years are enough to signify a shift in America's long-term view is unclear.

As Trump calls for global pullback, the US military designated Russia and China as the two greatest threats to the US. The case for Russia is clear, with its history of military aggression, most recently in Ukraine and Crimea, and its ongoing violation of weapons treaties. Its ongoing involvement in cyber attacks and election meddling suggests the threat remains real, especially as Russia pushes aggressively forward with its missile capabilities.

The outlook with respect to China is less clear. The US military, supported by the military industrial complex, is always looking for the next threat and the next generation of weapons. The facts behind the China threat are far less compelling than Russia. China's defense budget is growing at a slightly faster rate than in the US, but under one third the size despite the population being four times larger.[12] While China is more aggressive with respect to its territorial waters, its actions are benign by any measure compared to Russia and the US over the past five decades.

Can it be argued that, after years of waiting in the wings, China is ready to start flexing its muscles by leveraging hard and soft power? Of course. But military aggression would run counter to both its Confucian values and China's deeply rooted pragmatism. What foreign aggression by any country in the past 150 years created sustained value for the aggressor? Whatever examples China could come up with would be dwarfed in number and scale by those in which the aggressor ultimately paid a high price.

Will China fiercely defend its territory, including the islands disputed with Japan, the Philippines and Vietnam? Yes. The Chinese people are keenly aware of the 'Century of Humiliation', a period of Western power intervention and imperialism between 1839 and 1949, which is taught in every school.[13] But, with the eradication of poverty becoming a reality, the importance of stability and national pride is becoming more central. Defensive actions, however, are fundamentally different than aggression.

Some would argue, as in the Thucydides Trap, which says war between a leading global power and a rising global power is inevitable, that even if neither side sought war, a series of lesser events could lead to an unforeseen escalation.[14] Given the discipline and execution skills China demonstrated over the last 30 years since Tiananmen Square, and the collective experience of senior government officials, 'accidents' leading China to stumble into war are far harder to imagine than in the US.

As Henry Kissinger said in his excellent book, *On China*, the likelihood of direct military engagement between the US and China is remote.[15] Will the two great powers compete? Of course, but it will be on the basis of economic and social issues. The history and culture of China is consistent with this view. The pragmatists in the US would agree.

CHAPTER
8

WHERE WE GO FROM HERE ...

"We should work hard to develop joint projects with the Chinese in areas where we have agreement. No single relationship will be more important to the peace and stability of the world in this century than the relationship between the United States and China."

– David Boren, author of *A Letter to America* and former US Senator

While most dialogue on the US–China relationship focuses on its differences, the two countries share much in common. They are the two strongest countries globally, one leading the West and the other leading the East. Both economies were fueled by an industrial revolution, the US in roughly 1870 and China in roughly 1980. They share many of the same domestic challenges: high debt, weak social safety net, an aging population, income inequality and a deteriorating environment. Often overlooked, the people share a number of personal characteristics: strong work ethic, ambition, teamwork, helpfulness and a sense of humour. Successfully solving core global issues requires cooperation between the two countries.

In the US, there is a disturbing amount of mistrust towards China that is rooted in common misunderstandings about Chinese history, culture and government. This mistrust is actively encouraged by the current US administration, as is evidenced by the speech given by Vice President Mike Pence on 4 October 2018 to the Hudson Institute. I will not go into extensive detail about its contents other than to say his perspectives and arguments were neither balanced nor fact-based, and we should hope future presidential administrations after Trump's express a far stronger interest in understanding China as a country, government and people.[1]

The core objective of this book is to address these misunderstandings. There are certainly realities about China that make Americans uncomfortable, which I believe makes people in the US less likely to interact with China as a country and as a people. While these were all covered in greater detail earlier, I'd like to touch on a couple put forth by the US in an attempt to better explain the circumstances.

- *The assertion that China will eventually adopt a democracy.* Obviously none of us, including China, know what the future will bring. However, China has maintained a strong central government throughout the course of its long history, including over a dozen central governments which fell because they lost the support of the people. Whether that was due to some combination of lack of protection against invaders, inadequate response to famine and natural disasters, or high taxes and corruption, the strong central government model was retained when new leadership took over. Predicting a shift to democracy belies the reality of China's history and culture.

- *The Chinese people are suffering from a lack of human rights and will demand democracy.* The reality is the Chinese people are more supportive of their government than any other major country, in part because the government has delivered not only prosperity and stability but a high level of personal freedom. This is not to say the Chinese people are all content with the degree of personal freedoms they currently have. Constraints on freedom of speech, the press and assembly result in a level of unrest and protest, especially in large cities across China. Whether or not these freedoms will continue to expand over time is yet to be seen, but there has been significant progress.

- *China is unfair to the US on trade and stole America's intellectual property.* In short, this is correct. The Chinese are transparent about the fact that they do what is in China's best interest and expect other countries to do the same. Even President Trump, while visiting Beijing, said, "We have a trade problem or, more specifically, the US has a trade problem." In other words, the US negotiated a deal favourable to the Chinese and must address that through trade negotiations. However, the US can't blame China for negotiating the best deal possible. In terms of US IP theft, it's up to every country and corporation to protect its assets.

Until very recently the US did little in this regard. If we go back to its industrial revolution, it similarly took advantage of Great Britain's IP. The solution here demands that the US up its efforts to protect what is undoubtedly one of its most valuable resources.

- *China will become militarily aggressive.* Not only would war between the US and China be completely irrational and devastating for both sides, but China has a long history of non-violence and is unlikely to deviate from that. The fact that China is working to become a strong economic power might feel like a threat to the US, but does not make it a military threat. The only aggressive action China has recently taken is building a base in the South China Sea, which shouldn't antagonize the US considering it has bases in Guam, Korea and Japan, while China has no military bases elsewhere.

On the flip side, China has a far greater understanding of the US, which is driven by its extensive exposure through education and tourism. Over 26 million Chinese have visited the US, an impressive number when compared to fewer than one million Americans who have visited China.[2] The Chinese also take advantage of America's superior higher education system, which results in the Chinese accounting for approximately one third of international students in the US, including many government officials, educated in the US.[3] In fact, it is mandatory that senior government officials study American history, culture and attitudes at the Party School. This increased exposure means that, at present day, China has a far greater understanding of the US than the US does of China.

So, if the greatest barrier to the US and China cooperating is the lack of understanding of China, what are the root causes? They are grounded in the central idea that China's history and culture are unique, as are the US's, and that leads to two very different, but successful, models. These are what I view to be the biggest issues behind the lack of American trust in the Chinese.

- Perhaps most fundamental is the question of motives behind the senior leaders of the Chinese Communist Party. Is it, as *Dictator's Dilemma* author Bruce Dickson asserts, to retain its position of power? Or is it serving the people? For most authoritarian regimes, the evidence of self-serving and staying in power is overwhelming.[4] A few things indicate this is not the case in China. A high (60 %) turnover of the Central Committee roughly every five years is triggered by term limits and forced retirement age. The turnover undermines the notion of an entrenched, self-serving senior team that characterizes most authoritarian regimes. Since the CCP took over, the standard of living increased dramatically across China and over 850 million people were brought out of poverty. The level of prosperity the government achieved for China is remarkable and its approval ratings are high; neither of these things can be debated. Does the government overstep sometimes? Is there corruption within the Party, even if we can't see it? Of course, but that the CCP has accomplished a great deal on behalf of all of China beyond its rise to power is irrefutable.
- The acceptance of a collectivist vs. individualistic value system is critical. Skeptics will assert that a collectivistic view is an excuse for an authoritarian government to trample on the rights of individuals. However, Confucian values of family, serving society, education, morality, respect and modesty have shaped China for 2,500 years. Their importance in

shaping China into a collectivistic country cannot be overstated, and for the US to dismiss collectivism as an excuse for the government to behave in a way different from its own shows very little grounding in China's long historical and cultural evolution.

- The acceptance of meritocracy as a legitimate alternative for selecting leaders. The well documented and executed process involves disciplined performance review, examination results and peer voting. Since this selection process occurs behind closed doors, it is fair to question the legitimacy of these selections; we simply have no way of knowing because the information isn't public. However, the legitimacy of US government officials who access massive campaign contributions through 'donations' from influential organizations (like the NRA) and companies (like big oil) can be called into question in the same way. The only difference is, in the US, all of this information is public, though little has been done to address it.

- The 'Communist' label leads many Americans to equate China to Russia, though Russia's track record of military aggression and self-serving distribution of national wealth to political leaders and cronies is radically different than China's.

- Western literature is full of anti-China sentiments. *America's Coming War with China* by Ted Galen Carpenter asserts, as the title suggests, that war between the two powers is inevitable,[5] as does *Destined for War: Can America and China Escape Thucydides's Trap?* by Graham Allison.[6] *The Hundred Year Marathon* by Michael Pillsbury suggests that China has been planning to undermine the US and become number one by the 100-year anniversary of the Communist takeover in 2049.[7] This literature contributes to the negative impression many Americans have of China.

- How much of anti-China sentiment stems from the US fear of slipping behind China as the world's largest economy? While it can't be ignored that China works very hard to compete in the global market and was unnervingly successful at catching up with the US very quickly, this idea of winners and losers is unproductive. Is China competing with the US? Certainly, but the notion of 'winning' speaks to Western dualistic ideas and its own nervousness as a global power, and it doesn't necessarily reflect the motivation behind China's rise. Regardless of what those motivations are, it will certainly be hard to accomplish a win/win in this situation if the West cannot move beyond the idea of win/lose.

- The Western media, longstanding champion of human rights and individualism, consistently takes a negative position on China. Since Americans don't have much exposure to China and the Chinese people beyond Western media, they have little else to go on.

Given the weight of these root causes affecting the way Americans view China, what can be done to begin closing the gap? Here are a few examples of things I believe are critical to Americans overcoming this broad misunderstanding.

- Increase American exposure to China. Most Americans who spend a significant amount of time in China develop a largely balanced and positive view of China. A few prominent examples include Henry Kissinger, Hank Paulson, former Treasury Secretary who began strategic conversations with China,

Hank Greenberg, former Chairman of AIG who was the American who opened up the Chinese market for financial services, and the journalist Thomas Friedman. While travel to China is increasing and Mandarin is rapidly becoming a major foreign language in the US, there is still progress to be made in terms of cultural exchanges and joint collaborations between the two communities.

- China is consistently transparent when stating it has and will continue to act in the country's and people's best interest and expects nothing less from other countries. From this perspective, the US should never be surprised by the motivation behind China's actions.

- American organizations are expressing vocal concern about tariffs as well as restrictions on visas and immigration. Raising the heat on the US government while continuing to pressure China into opening its markets would accelerate joint understanding and cooperation. Corporate America is helpful on these issues.

- Educating Americans on doing business in China needs to go beyond business card protocal and manners to understand the more fundamental cultural issues. Examples include the importance of face and avoiding conflict, the difference between the Chinese indirect and American direct approaches, communicating and the Chinese patience/persistence.

- Finally, the US should resist the temptation to advise China on how it should change. Such advice comes off as arrogant, self-serving and hypocritical given that the US would never be receptive to advice from China.

The Chinese could also do much to help bridge this divide as well.

- Opening Chinese markets at an accelerated pace would ease tensions on both sides. Given the growing maturity of Chinese markets, the value of easing the tensions would more than compensate for the economic risk, if there even is any. Many would argue that American innovations would accelerate the development of Chinese markets, as smart phones have already done.
- While China rightfully says other countries should follow its lead in not interfering in other countries' internal affairs, China could temper internal actions that are red flags in the US and only marginally impact China. This includes the harsh treatment of dissidents, whose influence on China is largely inconsequential but whose persecution results in extremely negative press in the West. Neutralizing the Muslim terrorist threat is a global issue that many in the West understand, but the internment camps used in China result in many negative impressions in the West when there are numerous alternatives capable of accomplishing the same goal. While China reversed the recent decision to allow killing endangered rhinos and tigers, the damage was already done and could have been easily anticipated and avoided.
- Finally, joint projects to target global issues, as called for by David Boren, would go a long way to easing tensions and building mutual trust for the benefit of all. Others are far better equipped to identify the promising areas for collaboration than I, but the list of opportunities is undoubtedly long.

In an ideal world, more sensitivity and outreach and, ultimately, joint efforts on global issues is the right answer for everyone involved. Present day antagonizing and lack of collaboration on both sides is simultaneously frustrating and disheartening. If this collaboration doesn't happen it won't be the end of the world, especially for China, which has momentum on its side right now. US containment efforts are both too little, too late and counter-productive. The win/win for the world right now is mutual under-standing and respect between these two global powers, and the cooperation on global issues which would undoubtedly follow.

★ ★ ★

ENDNOTES

★ ★ ★

CHAPTER 1: CONTEXT

1. Naughton, Barry. *The Chinese Economy: Adaptation and Growth.* 2ʳᵈ ed., MIT Press, 2018. Print.

2. Weiping, Tan. *China's Approach to Reduce Poverty: Taking Targeted Measures to Lift People out of Poverty.* Addis Ababa: International Poverty Reduction Center in China, 2018. <https://www.un.org/development/desa/dspd/wp-content/uploads/sites/22/2018/05 /31.pdf>

3. "GDP Growth (annual %)." The World Bank, 2019. <https://data.worldbank.org/indicator/NY.GDP.MKTP.KD.ZG?end=2017&locations=GB-US-FR-DE-CN&start=1978>

4. See note 2 above

5. Wike, Richard. "Global Views on Life Satisfaction, National Conditions, and the Global Economy."The Pew Research Center: The Pew Global Attitudes Project, 2007. <http://www.pewresearch.org/wp-content/uploads/sites/2/2007/11/Pew-Global-Attitudes-11-5-07-release-_final_.pdf>

6. LI, CHENG, editor. *China's Changing Political Landscape: Prospects for Democracy.* Brookings Institution Press, 2008, <www.jstor.org/stable/10.7864/j.ctt6wpf6v.>

7. Upton-McLaughlin, Sean. *Gaining and Losing Face in China.* The China Culture Corner, 2013. <https://chinaculturecorner.com/2013/10/10/face-in-chinese-business/>

8. See note 2 above

9. Freije-Rodriguez, Samuel. "Poverty and Equity Brief, East Asia & Pacific: China. World Bank Group, 2018."

10. The Editors of Encyclopaedia Britannica. "Three Kingdoms." *Encyclopaedia Britannica*, 2018. <https://www.britannica.com/event/Three-Kingdoms-ancient-kingdoms-China>

CHAPTER 2: CULTURE

1. Boren, David. *A Letter To America.* Norman: University of Oklahoma Press, 2008. Print.

2. Kessler, Glenn. "Does the Trump tax cut give 83 percent of the benefits to the top 1 percent?" *The Washington Post*, 14 November 2018. <https://www.washingtonpost.com/politics/2018/11/14/does-trump-tax-cut-give-percent-benefits-top-one-percent/?utm_term=.a0e00cbbc7ee>

3. "Here's The Cost of War for Each Major Conflict in America's 239-Year History." *The Daily Caller*, 16 October 2015. https://dailycaller.com/2015/10/16/heres-the-cost-of-war-for-each-major-conflict-in-americas-239-year-history/

CHAPTER 3: ECONOMIC PERFORMANCE

1. "Households and NPISHs Final consumption expenditure per capita (constant 2010 US$)." The World Bank, 2019. <https://data.worldbank.org/indicator/NE.CON.PRVT.PC.KD>

2. Li, Zhou and Chongqing Ren. "Agriculture Transition in China: Experiences and Lessons." *Wieś i Rolnictwo*, 2014, nr 3(164), pp. 25-44.

3. See chapter 1 note 1

4. Woetzel, Jonathan et al. *Bridging Global Infrastructure Gaps*. McKinsey & Company: McKinsey Global Institute, June 2016. <https://www.mckinsey.com/~/media/McKinsey/Industries/Capital%20Projects%20and%20Infrastructure/Our%20Insights/Bridging%20global%20infrastructure%20gaps/Bridging-Global-Infrastructure-Gaps-Full-report-June-2016.ashx>

5. Mozur, Paul. "Beijing Wants A.I. to Be Made in China by 2030." *The New York Times*, 20 July 2017. <https://www.nytimes.com/2017/07/20/business/china-artificial-intelligence.html>

6. Huang, Yukon. *Cracking the China Conundrum: Why Conventional Economic Wisdom is Wrong*. New York: Oxford University Press, 2017. Print.

7. "Urban population (% of total)" *The World Bank*, 2018. <https://data.worldbank.org/indicator/SP.URB.TOTL.IN.ZS>

8. "Consumption contributes to nearly 80% of China's GDP growth." *China Daily*, 20 September 2018. <http://global.chinadaily.com.cn/a/201809/20/WS5ba30475a310c4cc775e7413.html>

9. "Services, value added (% of GDP)." The World Bank, 2019. <https://data.worldbank.org/indicator/NV.SRV.TOTL.ZS>

10. "Meeting China's productivity challenge." McKinsey Global Institute, August 2016. <https://www.mckinsey.com/featured-insights/china/meeting-chinas-productivity-challenge>

11. "Current Healthcare expenditure (% GDP)." The World Bank, 2019. <https://data.worldbank.org/indicator/SH.XPD.CHEX.GD.ZS?locations=CN-US&name_desc=false>

12. Nayyar, Sarita et al. *Future of Consumption in Fast-Growth Consumer Markets: China*. World Economic Forum, 2018. <http://www3.weforum.org/docs/WEF_Future_of_Consumption_in_Fast_Growth_Consumer_Markets_China.pdf>

13. Wang, Orange. "Beijing's tilt towards state-owned enterprises raises doubts about future of private sector in Chinese economy." *South China Morning Post*, 21 Sept. 2018 <https://www.scmp.com/news/article/2165254/beijings-tilt-towards-state-owned-enterprises-raises-doubts-about-future>

14. Farrell, Diana and Susan Lund. "Putting China's capital to work." McKinsey & Company, Far Eastern Economic Review, 1 May 2006. <https://www.mckinsey.com/mgi/overview/in-the-news /putting-chinas-capital-to-work>

15. "China Net Household Saving Rate." *Trading Economics*, 2019. <https://tradingeconomics.com/china/personal-savings>

16. "Personal saving rate in the United States from 1960 to 2018." *Statistica*, 2019. <https://www.statista.com/statistics/246234/personal-savings-rate-in-the-united-states/>

17. "$1B+ Market Map: The World's 326 Unicorn Companies In One Infographic." *CB Insights*, 14 March 2019. <https://www.cbinsights.com/research/unicorn-startup-market-map/>

18. Huang, Yukon. *Cracking the China Conundrum: Why Conventional Economic Wisdom is Wrong*. New York: Oxford University Press, 2017. Print.

19. McKinsey Global Insights Article: "China and the World: Inside a changing economic relationship." McKinsey & Company, December 2019. Print.

20. "China Current Account to GDP." *Trading Economics*, 2019. <https://tradingeconomics.com/china/current-account-to-gdp>

21. "Tariff rate, applied, weighted mean, all products (%)" The World Bank, 2019. <https://data.worldbank.org/indicator/TM.TAX.MRCH.WM.AR.ZS>

22. Saiidi, Uptin. "China's foreign direct investment into the US dropped precipitously in 2018, data show." *CNBC*, 15 January 2019. <https://www.cnbc.com/2019/01/15/chinese-foreign-direct-investment-to-the-us-falls-in-2018-data.html>

23. "What happens when Chinese students abroad return home." *The Economist*, 17 May 2018. <https://www.economist.com/special-report/2018/05/17/what-happens-when-chinese-students-abroad-return-home>

24. "Full List." *Fortune 500*, 2018. <http://fortune.com/fortune500/>

25. See chapter 1 note 1

26. Normile, Dennis. "Surging R&D spending in China narrows gap with United States." *Science Magazine*, 10 October 2018. <https://www.sciencemag.org/news/2018/10/surging-rd-spending-china-narrows-gap-united-states>

27. "Share of old age population (65 years and older) in the total U.S. population from 1950 to 2050*." Statistica, 2019. <https://www.statista.com/ statistics/457822/share-of-old-age-population-in-the- total-us-population/>

28. China Power Team. "Does China have an aging problem?" *ChinaPower*, 15 February 2016. <https://chinapower.csis.org/aging-problem/>

29. Mourdoukoutas, Panos. "Debt, Not Trade War, Is China's Biggest Problem." *Forbes Magazine*, 24 November 2018. <https://www.forbes.com/sites/panosmourdoukoutas/2018/11/24/ debt-not-trade-war- is-chinas-biggest-problem/#517dfb6b4c4d>

CHAPTER 4: EDUCATION SYSTEMS

1. "Facts and Studies." *Council for American Private Education*, 2019. <http://www.capenet.org/facts.html>

2. Radensky, Andre. "Made in China 2025." *Business Today Online Journal, Business Today Online Journal*, 10 October 2018, <journal.businesstoday.org/bt-online/2018/made-in-china-2025>

3. Ministry of Education of the People's Republic of China. "Vocational Education in China." China.org, 20 October 2006. <http://www.china.org.cn/english/LivinginChina/185280.htm>

4. Strauss, Valerie. "Where in the world are teachers most respected? Not in the U.S., a new survey shows." *The Washington Post*, 15 Nov 2018. <https://www.washingtonpost.com/ education/2018/11/15/where-world- are-teachers-most-respected-not-us-new-survey-shows/?utm_term=. a5c46ab47975>

5. "Estimated average annual salary of teachers in public elementary and secondary schools, by state or jurisdiction: Selected years, 1969-70 through 2009-10." National Center for Educational Statistics, May 2010. <https://nces.ed.gov/programs/digest/d10/tables/dt10_ 083.asp>

6. Anderson, Jenny. "Asians spend seven times as much as Americans on tutoring to give their kids an edge." *Quartz*, 27 April 2017. <https://qz.com/970130/asians-spend-15-of- their-family-income-on-extra- education-and-tutoring-for-kids-americans-spend-it-on-cars-and-gas/>

7. Quacquarelli Symonds Staff. "The World's Top 100 Universities." Top Universities, 6 June 2018. <https://www.topuniversities.com/student- info/choosing-university/worlds-top-100-universities>

8. "Time in school: How does the U.S. compare?" Center for Public Education, December 2011.

9. Human Rights Advocate. "South Korea's commitment to invest in education pays off." *The World Top 20 Project*, 16 January 2018. <https://worldtop20.org/the-incredible-south-korean-education-system>

10. "People's Republic of China." Programme for International Student Assessment, 2015. <http://www.compareyourcountry.org/pisa/country/chn?lg=en>

11. Yan, Li. "China works hard to achieve its goal of spending 4 percent GDP on education." *People's Daily Online*, 22 September 2017. <http://en.people.cn/n3/2017/0922/c90000-9272722.html>

12. "Education at a Glance 2018: People's Republic of China." *ODEC Indicators*, 2018. http://gpseducation.oecd.org/Content/EAGCountryNotes/CHN.pdf

CHAPTER 5: HUMAN RIGHTS

1. Mervosh, Sarah. "Nearly 40,000 People Died From Guns in U.S. Last Year, Highest in 50 Years." *The New York Times*, 18 December 2018. <https://www.nytimes.com/2018/12/18/us/gun-deaths.html>

2. See chapter 1 note 2

3. "Life expectancy at birth, total (years)." The World Bank, 2019. <https://data.worldbank.org/indicator/SP.DYN.LE00.IN?locations=CN>

4. "Adult* literacy rate in China from 1982 to 2015." Statistica, 2019. <https://www.statista.com/statistics/271336/literacy-in-china/>

5. "Mortality rate, infant (per 1,000 live births)." The World Bank, 2019. <https://data.worldbank.org/indicator/SP.DYN.IMRT.IN?locations=CN>

6. de Tocqueville, Alexis. *Democracy in America*. London: The University of Chicago Press, 2000. Print.

7. See chapter 1 note 1

8. "Number of students from China that have studied abroad between 2007 and 2017 (in thousands)." Statistica, 2019. <https://www.statista.com/statistics/227240/number-of-chinese-students-that-study-abroad/>

9. "What happens when Chinese students abroad return home." *The Economist*, 17 May 2018. <https://www.economist.com/special-report/2018/05/17/what-happens-when-chinese-students-abroad-return-home>

10. Wu, Xiaogang; Cheng, Jinhua. "The Emerging New Middle Class and the Rule of Law in China." Chinese University Press: China Review, Vol. 13, No. 1 (Spring 2013), pp. 43-70.

11. "The Most Litigious Countries in the World." Clements Worldwide. <https://www.clements.com/sites/default/files/resources/The-Most-Litigious-Countries-in-the-World.pdf>

12. Gao, Jie. "Comparison Between Chinese and American Lawyers: Educated and Admitted to Practice Differently in Different Legal Systems." *Penn State International Law Review*: Vol. 29: No. 1, (2010) Article 11.

13. *Peoples Republic of China Constitution*. Art. 13, 21, 24. 2004.

14. "Race and Ethnicity in the U.S." The Statistical Atlas, 4 September 2018. <https://statisticalatlas.com/United-States/Race-and-Ethnicity>

15. Kochhar, Rakesh and Anthony Cilluffo. "Incomes of whites, blacks, Hispanics and Asians in the U.S., 1970 and 2016." The Pew Research Center, 12 July 2018. <http://www.pewsocialtrends.org/2018/07/12/incomes-of-whites-blacks-hispanics-and-asians-in-the-u-s-1970-and-2016/>

16. Tate, Emily. "Graduation Rates and Race." *Inside Higher Ed*, 26 April 2017. <https://www.insidehighered.com/news/2017/04/26/college-completion-rates-vary-race-and-ethnicity-report-finds>

17. "Labor force characteristics by race and ethnicity, 2017." Bureau of Labor Statistics, August 2018. <https://www.bls.gov/opub/reports/race-and-ethnicity/2017/home.htm>

18. "CRIMINAL JUSTICE FACT SHEET." NAACP, 2019. <https://www.naacp.org/criminal-justice-fact-sheet/>

19. See note 14 above

20. See note 15 above

21. See note 14 above

22. See note 15 above

23. "Facts for Features: Hispanic Heritage Month 2017." United States Census Bureau, 31 August 2017. <https://www.census.gov/newsroom/facts-for-features/2017/hispanic-heritage.html>

24. Shammas, Brittany. "Miami Is Only U.S. City Where Most Language Learners Are Studying English." *Miami New Times*, 13 October 2017. <https://www.miaminewtimes.com/news/miami-is-only-us-city-where-most-studied-language-is-english-9743341>

25. Lee, Tanya. "7 Apologies Made to American Indians." *Indian Country Today*, 1 July 2015. <https://newsmaven.io/indiancountrytoday/archive/7-apologies-made-to-american-indians-CzHzxFZyVk6QdDF-Naiyyw/>

26. Jacobs, Andrew. "Olympic Official Calls Protests a 'Crisis'.." *The New York Times*, 11 April 2008. <https://www.nytimes.com/2008/04/11/world/asia/11china.html>

27. "China Steps Up Crackdown Of Tibet Protests." *CBS News*, 20 March 2008. <https://www.cbsnews.com/news/china-steps-up-crackdown-of-tibet-protests/>

28. "Self-immolations by Tibetans." International Campaign for Tibet, 10 December 2018. <https://www.savetibet.org/resources/fact-sheets/self-immolations-by-tibetans/>

29. Branigan, Tania. "Ethnic violence in China leaves 140 dead." *The Guardian*, 6 July 2009. https://www.theguardian.com/world/2009/jul/06/china-riots-uighur-xinjiang

30. Kaiman, Jonathan. "Islamist group claims responsibility for attack on China's Tiananmen Square." *The Guardian*, 25 Nov 2013. <https://www.theguardian.com/world/2013/nov/25/islamist-china-tiananmen-beijing-attack>

31. "China mass stabbing: Deadly knife attack in Kunming." *BBC News*, 2 March 2014. <https://www.bbc.com/news/world-asia-china-26402367>

32. Sudworth, John. "China's hidden camps: What's happened to the vanished Uighurs of Xinjiang?" *BBC World News*, 2018. <https://www.bbc.co.uk/news/resources/idt-sh/China_hidden_camps>

33. Liddicoat, Anthony (ed.). *Language Planning and Policy: Issues in Language Planning and Literacy*. Multilingual Matters, 5 July 2007. Print.

34. See chapter 1 note 2

35. See chapter 1 note 1

36. CNN Library. "LGBT Rights Milestones Fast Facts." *CNN*, 22 January 2019. <https://www.cnn.com/2015/06/19/us/lgbt-rights-milestones-fast-facts/index.html>

37. Speelman, Tabitha. "Tiptoeing Out of the Closet: The History and Future of LGBT Rights in China." *The Atlantic*, 21 August 2013. <https://www.theatlantic.com/china/archive/2013/08/tiptoeing-out-of-the-closet-the-history-and-future-of-lgbt-rights-in-china/278869/>

38. Palmer, James. "It's Still (Just About) OK to Be Gay in China." *Foreign Policy*, 17 April 2018. <https://foreignpolicy.com/2018/04/17/its-still-just-about-ok-to-be-gay-in-china/>

39. "Religion in America: U.S. Religious Data, Demographics and Statistics." Pew Research Center, 2019. <http://www.pewforum.org/religious-landscape-study/>

40. Faison, Seth. "In Beijing: A Roar of Silent Protesters." *The New York Times*, 27 April 1999. <https://archive.nytimes.com/www.nytimes.com/library/world/asia/042799china-protest.html>

41. "The Global Religious Landscape: A Report on the Size and Distribution of the World's Major Religious Groups as of 2010." The Pew Research Center, December 2010. <http://assets.pewresearch.org/wp-content/uploads/sites/11/2014/01/global-religion-full.pdf>

42. Milligan, Susan. "Stepping Through History: A timeline of women's rights from 1769 to the 2017 Women's March on Washington." *U.S. News*, 20 January 2017. <https://www.usnews.com/news/the-report/articles/2017-01-20/timeline-the-womens-rights-movement-in-the-us>

43. "The Data on Women Leaders." Pew Research Center, January 2015. Updated Jan 2019. <http://www.pewsocialtrends.org/fact-sheet/the-data-on-women-leaders/>

44. Warner, Judith et al. "The Women's Leadership Gap." Center for American Progress, 20 November 2018. <https://www.americanprogress.org/issues/women/reports/2018/11/20/461273/womens-leadership-gap-2/>

45. Denyer, Simon; Gowen, Annie. "Too many men: China and India battle with the consequences of gender imbalance." *South China Morning Post: Post Magazine*, 24 April 2018. <https://www.scmp.com/magazines/post-magazine/long-reads/article/2142658/too-many-men-china-and-india-battle-consequences>

46. "Adult* literacy rate in China from 1982 to 2015." Statistica, 2019. <https://www.statista.com/statistics/271336/literacy-in-china/>

47. Sun J.Y., Li J. (2017). "Women in Leadership in China: Past, Present, and Future." In: Cho Y., Ghosh R., Sun J., McLean G. (eds), *Current Perspectives on Asian Women in Leadership. Current Perspectives on Asian Women in Leadership.* Palgrave Macmillan, Cham.

CHAPTER 6: FORMS OF DEMOCRACY

1. Panetta, Gracie; Reaney, Olivia. "The evolution of American voting rights in 242 years shows how far we've come — and how far we still have to go." *Business Insider*, 15 February 2019. <https://www.businessinsider.com/when-women-got-the-right-to-vote-american-voting-rights-timeline-2018-10>

2. Albert, Zachary. "Trends in Campaign Finance, 1980-2016." Campaign Finance Task Force, 12 October 2017. <https://bipartisanpolicy.org/wp-content/uploads/2018/02/Trends-in-Campaign-Financing-1980-2016.-Zachary-Albert..pdf>

3. Confessor, Nicholas. "$2 Billion Worth of Free Media for Donald Trump." *The New York Times*, 15 March 2016. <https://www.nytimes.com/2016/03/16/upshot/measuring-donald-trumps-mammoth-advantage-in-free-media.html>

4. Desilver, Drew. "U.S. trails most developed countries in voter turnout." *The Pew Research Center*, 21 May 2018. <http://www.pewresearch.org/fact-tank/2018/05/21/u-s-voter-turnout-trails-most-developed-countries/>

5. Ibid.

6. Chokshi, Niraj. "Map: The most Democratic and Republican states." *The Washington Post*, 6 February 2015. <https://www.washingtonpost.com/blogs/govbeat/wp/2015/02/06/map-the-most-democratic-and-republican-states/?utm_term=.91e4d1804a61>

7. File, Thom. "Voting in America: A Look at the 2016 Presidential Election." *United States Census Bureau*, 10 May 2017. <https://www.census.gov/newsroom/blogs/random-samplings/2017/05/voting_in_america.html>

8. Boren, David. *A Letter To America*. University of Oklahoma Press, 1 May 2011. Print.

9. Kessler, Glenn. "Does the Trump tax cut give 83 percent of the benefits to the top 1 percent?" *The Washington Post*, 14 November 2018. <https://www.washingtonpost.com/politics/2018/11/14/does-trump-tax-cut-give-percent-benefits-top-one-percent/?utm_term=.a0e00cbbc7ee>

10. Saad, Lydia. "Perceived Need for Third Major Party Remains High in U.S." *The Gallup Poll*, 27 September 2017. <https://news.gallup.com/poll/219953/perceived-need-third-major-party-remains-high.aspx>

11. Wilson, Megan. "The NRA's power: By the numbers." *The Hill*, 8 October 2017. <https://thehill.com/business-a-lobbying/business-a-lobbying/354317-the-nras-power-by-the-numbers>

12. Ingraham, Christopher. "The richest 1 percent now owns more of the country's wealth than at any time in the past 50 years." *The Washington Post*, 6 December 2017. <https://www.washingtonpost.com/news/wonk/wp/2017/12/06/the-richest-1-percent-now-owns-more-of-the-countrys-wealth-than-at-any-time-in-the-past-50-years/?utm_term=.20b9eb5bae47>

13. Bach, Natasha. "Most Americans Support Increasing Taxes on the Wealthy: Poll." *Fortune Media LP*, 4 February 2019. <http://fortune.com/2019/02/04/support-for-tax-increase-on-wealthy-americans-poll/>

14. "Voters Blame Politicians for Federal Deficit." *Rasmussen Reports*, 21 February 2018. <http://www.rasmussenreports.com/public_content/politics/general_politics/february_2018/voters_blame_politicians_for_federal_deficit>

15. McCarthy, Niall. "The Top 15 Countries For Military Expenditure In 2016 [Infographic]." *Forbes Magazine*, 24 April 2017. <https://www.forbes.com/sites/niallmccarthy/2017/04/24/the-top-15-countries-for-military-expenditure-in-2016-infographic/#50a68b4143f3>

16. Gotoff, Daniel; Lake, Celinda. "Voters Want Criminal Justice Reform. Are Politicians Listening?" *The Marshall Project*, 13 November 2018. <https://www.themarshallproject.org/2018/11/13/voters-want-criminal-justice-reform-are-politicians-listening>

17. "The Evolving Landscape of Crime and Incarceration." Greenberg Quinlan Rosner Research, 19 April 2018. <https://storage.googleapis.com/vera-web-assets/inline-downloads/iob-poll-results-summary.pdf>

18. See chapter 4 note 18

19. See note 16 above

20. "Public Opinion Favors Criminal Justice and Drug Policy Reform, Making Now the Time to Act." Legal Action Center, November 2015. <https://lac.org/public-opinion-favors-criminal-justice-and-drug-policy-reform-making-now-the-time-to-act/>

21. "Having Chinese Communist Party membership is like having 'a diploma', 'opens doors'." *The Straits Time*, 21 October 2017. <https://www.straitstimes.com/asia/east-asia/having-chinese-communist-party-membership-is-like-having-a-diploma-and-opens-doors>

22. "2018 Edelman Trust Barometer: Global Report." Edelman, 2018. <https://www.edelman.com/sites/g/files/aatuss191/files/2018-10/2018_Edelman_Trust_Barometer_Global_Report_FEB.pdf>

23. Ibid.

CHAPTER 7: WORLDVIEW AND THE MILITARY

1. Cartwright, Mark. "Ancient Korean & Chinese Relations." *Ancient History Encyclopedia*, 30 November 2016. <https://www.ancient.eu/article/984/ancient-korean--chinese-relations/>

2. Chan, Minnie. "Border war with Vietnam a lingering wound for China's forgotten soldiers." *South China Morning Post*, 17 February 2019. <https://www.scmp.com/news/china/military/article/2186515/veterans-chinas-war-vietnam-say-they-are-too-afraid-remember>

3. "Here's the Cost of War for Each Major Conflict in America's 239-Year History." *The Daily Caller*, 16 October 2015. <https://dailycaller.com/2015/10/16/heres-the-cost-of-war-for-each-major-conflict-in-americas-239-year-history/>

4. Keller, Josh, et al. "Tracking Trump's Agenda, Step by Step." *The New York Times*, 26 January 2017. <www.nytimes.com/interactive/2017/us/politics/trump-agenda-tracker.html>

5. Taylor, Adam. "What Is the Monroe Doctrine? John Bolton's Justification for Trump's Push against Maduro." *The Washington Post*, 4 March 2019. <www.washingtonpost.com/world/2019/03/04/what-is-monroe-doctrine-john-boltons-justification-trumps-push-against-maduro/?noredirect=on&utm_term=.b5f49b1b0af7>

6. Wang, Q. Edward. "History, Space, and Ethnicity: The Chinese Worldview." University of Calgary, 1997. <www.people.ucalgary.ca/~slchia/article.html>

7. Zhang, Yongjin. "The Tribute System." Oxford Bibliographies, Oxford Bibliographies, 22 Apr. 2013, <www.oxfordbibliographies.com/view/document/obo-9780199920082/obo-9780199920082-0069.xml>

8. Edwards, Jim. "500 Years Ago, China Destroyed Its World-Dominating Navy Because Its Political Elite Was Afraid of Free Trade." *The Independent*, 8 March 2017. <www.independent.co.uk/news/world/americas/500-years-ago-china-destroyed-its-world-dominating-navy-because-its-political-elite-was-afraid-of-a7612276.html>

9. He, Mike. "Chinese History | A 5,000 Year Timeline of Events by China Mike." *China Mike*, 22 June 2017. <www.china-mike.com/chinese-history-timeline/>

10. "Ethnicity and Race by Countries." Infoplease, Sandbox Networks Inc, <www.infoplease.com/ethnicity-and-race-countries>

11. Radensky, Andre. "Made in China 2025." Business Today Online Journal, Business Today Online Journal, 10 Oct. 2018, <www.journal.businesstoday.org/bt-online/2018/made-in-china-2025.>

12. "What Does China Really Spend on Its Military?" *ChinaPower*, 9 October 2018. <www.chinapower.csis.org/military-spending/>

13. Lee, Andy S. "A Century of Humiliation: Understanding the Chinese Mindset." *The McGill International Review*, 18 February 2018. <www.mironline.ca/century-humiliation-understanding-chinese-mindset/>

14. Allison, Graham. "The Thucydides Trap." *Foreign Policy*, 9 June 2017. <www.foreignpolicy.com/2017/06/09/the-thucydides-trap/>

15. Kissinger, Henry. *On China*. Penguin Books, 2012. Print.

CHAPTER 8: WHERE WE GO FROM HERE ...

1. Pence, Mike. "The Administration's Policy Towards China." Hudson Institute, New York City, October 4 Event, 4 October 2018.. <www.hudson.org/events/1610-vice-president-mike-pence-s-remarks-on-the-administration-s-policy-towards-china102018.>

2. "International Visitations to the U.S. from China." 2017 International Inbound Travel Market Profile, U.S. Travel Association, 2017, <www.ustravel.org/system/files/media_root/document/Research_Country-Profile_2017_China.pdf>

3. Struck, Kathleen. "US Officials Warn of Chinese Influence in American Higher Education." *VOA*, 4 October 2018, <www.voanews.com/a/us-officials-warn-of-chinese-influence-in-american-higher-education/4600204.html>

4. Dickson, Bruce. *The Dictator's Dilemma: The Chinese Communist Party's Strategy for Survival*. Oxford University Press, 2016. Print.

5. Carpenter, Ted Galen. *America's Coming War with China: A Collision Course over Taiwan*. 1st ed., St. Martin's Press, 2015. Print.

6. Allison, Graham. *Destined for War: Can America and China Escape Thucydides's Trap?* Houghton Mifflin Harcourt, 2015. Print.

7. Pillsbury, Michael. *Hundred-Year Marathon*. Griffin, 2016. Print.

ABOUT THE AUTHOR

Photo by Christina Gundersen

Peter B. Walker is a Senior Partner Emeritus at McKinsey&Co, the world's leading management consultancy firm. During his 46 years at the firm, he worked with a wide range of financial institutions around the world, with a focus on China.

★ ★ ★

BOOK SUMMARY

★ ★ ★

From Trump's aggressive rhetoric against China, to the escalating trade war with tit for tat responses and China's 2025 initiative that threatens the US global leadership in advanced technologies, tensions between the two dominant forces of today's world have never been higher.

Each country's model is deeply rooted in their respective histories and cultures, with both models proving highly successful in achieving their main goals and highly resilient over time. This timely analysis of the US-China relationship explores the core misconceptions on governance, economic, social and military issues, and the root causes of these misconceptions. The author argues that if China and the US could close the gap by each understanding these differences and their implications, they could work together to overcome global issues to the benefit of all.